Amazing Graces

Pre-Prandial
WORDS OF
Spiritual Uplift
TO GRACE ANY
Gathering

The Very Reverend William J. Morris

MINISTER OF GLASGOW CATHEDRAL

FOREWORD BY RONNIE CORBETT

www.vitalspark.co.uk

The Vital Spark is an imprint of
Neil Wilson Publishing Ltd
303a The Pentagon Centre
36 Washington Street
GLASGOW
G3 8AZ

Tel: 0141-221-1117
Fax: 0141-221-5363
E-mail: info@nwp.sol.co.uk
http://www.nwp.co.uk

A catalogue record for this book is available from the British Library.
Illustrations © Bill Ferguson, 2001.

ISBN 1-903238-35-8
Typeset in Aldine
Designed by Robbie Porteous
Printed by WS Bookwell

Amazing Graces

Contents

Foreword

I have to say that I do attend an uneasy number of formal, charitable, and, I am sure, highly worthy black-tie dinners. Sometimes I am to speak myself, though I do try to limit these, but if I am not performing I am certainly going to have to listen, sometimes at length (a bit wearisome) but mostly I enjoy myself.

There is a very important moment in all of these evenings that is often awkwardly or perhaps even crudely handled. I mean of course ... the Grace. In order to make it seem appropriate and very contemporary, it can become a bit lumpy and self-conscious. When it is deftly handled, with a light touch and gentle humour, it is always memorable. And when it is delivered in rhyme as well, it is a classic moment. The Very Reverend William Morris of Glasgow Cathedral is probably *the* expert in this style at this time. (I have to say that the late Archbishop of Canterbury, Robert Runcie, had the same graceful, but everyday touch.)

This book is a collection of such graces and a record of such moments and I commend it to you. Enjoy it, as I did.

Ronnie Corbett

Preface

In The Beginning ...

When I came to Glasgow in the autumn of 1967 Alastair Warren, then editor of the *Glasgow Herald*, invited me out to lunch. As we talked about Glasgow and the Cathedral, I remarked that on the previous Thursday evening, the shops being open late, I had met in succession in Sauchiehall Street a Baillie on Glasgow Corporation, the Deacon Convener of the Trades of Glasgow, one of my Cathedral elders and a friend from Peterhead doing 15 years for culpable homicide, but out on pre-Training for Freedom leave.

Alastair agreed that Glasgow was a very friendly place, rather like a large village, he said, grown as it was from a number of smaller burghs. He went on to say that his father had told him that the Lord Provost, the Deacon Convener, the editor of the *Glasgow Herald*, and the Minister of the Cathedral were the four best-fed men in Glasgow because of the number of dinners to which they were all invited.

Our Lord Himself seems to have had a fairly wide-ranging social life being a guest of Pharisees and village families and a welcome friend of the socially and politically incorrect outcasts of the society of His day. He contrasted His reputation with that of John the Baptist, the latter being regarded by some people as abnormally unsociable while others thought Jesus was sociable to excess.

This book could not have appeared without the kind hospitality of many organisations, friends and their families whose names appear in it. Many of them have for years suggested that a book like this be published. I am grateful to them all for their continuing generous support and friendship.

★★★

One evening about 25 years ago I was heading over the Kingston Bridge towards town from the southside, thinking of the grace that I had been asked to say.

Whatever the occasion, I had always tried to make it appropriate to the event, but it had never occurred to me to try to do one in rhyme.

This was the annual dinner of The Institute of Chartered Accountants of Scotland, which was held alternately in Glasgow and Edinburgh. It was at a time of economic restraint. The 'freeze' was a word in common parlance. As I drove on, thinking about the grace, I said to myself, 'This could easily be put into rhyme.' On arrival at my destination I sat in the car for a few moments and scribbled my grace on the back of the invitation card.

At such a convivial gathering numbering about 700 (mainly) men, young and old, mostly accountants or associated professions, the heart-warming process being long begun, and so the grace was usually very much a formality. This time, however, a greater than usual silence descended on the gathering as I proceeded. Gradually some appreciative chuckles emanated and as I concluded there was a tension-breaking gale of laughter and considerable applause. Thus my rhyming graces tradition started and has continued ever since. Almost always they have met with the same response.

Understandably, there are some who feel uncomfortable about laughter and applause as responses to anything said in a religious context. I usually preface my graces in public with the normal bidding – 'Let us pray', and I take the laughter or applause as an appropriate form of 'Amen' with its root meaning of 'support'.

I hope that everyone will read these graces with interest and perhaps with enjoyment, especially on the part of those who heard some of them as originally spoken.

***

I am especially indebted to Dr Archie Fleming who has kept me moving this project forward and to the Trades House of Glasgow and their distinguished clerk, Gordon Wylie, for their, as always, generous support.

***

To Jean and David

who heard them all before – and some after

1
The Trades House of Glasgow

The Trades House, created in 1605, is a federal union of fourteen Incorporations, equivalent to the craft guilds or livery companies in London and other cities. The original purpose was the maintenance of high standards of craftmanship, the welfare of craftsmen and their dependants.

The chairman of the House is the Deacon Convener, now elected for one year in office. Each incorporation is led by a Deacon, or Visitor in one case, and a Master Court.

Every year, the House and the Crafts disburse considerable funds to charitable causes including medical research and education, and help for the disabled. Pensioners who are relatives of former members of the House are supported, and prizes to encourage students to high levels of attainment are given each year.

Most of the Crafts trace their origins to the sixteenth century and several were given their charters by the Archbishops of Glasgow before the Reformation.

Visit of Her Majesty's High Commissioner to the General Assembly of the Church of Scotland to the Trades House of Glasgow[1]

Be with us, Lord, as here we meet
    The High Commissioner and her Suite,
And thank Thee for good food to eat.

Lord, bless her Grace in this her city.
    May she be moved to praise or pity,
Welcomed with words both wise and witty.

Bless Thou this House, renowned of old
    For craftsmen caring, skilled and bold.
By our deeds may their praise be told.

***

[1] Lady Marion Fraser, LT, LLD, Dundee University.
The Lord High Commissioner or, in the case of a lady, Her Majesty's High Commissioner, represents the Queen at the General Assembly of the Church of Scotland in May each year. In addition the High Commissioner entertains commissioners from the church and guests with hospitality in the Palace of Holyroodhouse and undertakes a programme of visits all over Scotland to organisations and institutions.
Lady Fraser was HM High Commissioner in 1994–5.

DEACON CONVENER'S DINNER

To men of old Thou gavest skill
    To build a ship, perhaps to till
The ground, or fashion shoes, or brew
    A malt to warm the heart. So through
Such skills this city grew, and then,
    Since they were wise and friendly men,
Their crafts made common cause at length
    And still proclaim, 'Union is Strength.'
Lord, bless their sons here and their guests.
    With joy and peace, grant their requests.

***

Lord Jesus, who Thyself once worked with skill:
    Be present with each craftsman here,
Inspire each guest.
    We thank Thee for these gifts of Thy good will.
May we, this House, and all our works
    By thee be blest.

***

Lord, who among us could find fault
    With one who helps produce the Malt.
Few ministers, Thy servants, shirk
    A dram, when offered, of Auld Kirk
So we look forward soon, or later,
    To sampling from a glass the Cratur.

But first, we pray Thee bless, O Lord,
    Thy gifts provided at this board.
'Praise be to God,' the Maltmen say,
    And each of us joins them to pray
That blessings from Convener Allan[2]
    May freely flow – gill, pint, or gallon.

[2] Allan Denholm, Deacon Convener 1998–9, was secretary and director of William Grant & Sons, Ltd; Visitor of the Incorporation of Maltmen, 1980–1; President of the Institute of Chartered Accountants of Scotland, 1992–3.

Some Deacon Conveners are sailors,
    Our new one may be, or not.
From the Incorporation of Tailors
    We pray Thou wilt bless, Lord, Roy Scott.[3]

As a surgeon skilful at sewing,
    With soluble stitches he's neat.
To Thee, as to him, Lord, we're owing
    Our thanks for the food we shall eat.

Bless the Master Courts here who now gather,
    The Trades House and each honoured guest.
To Thee, Lord, Creator and Father,
    For thy goodness our thanks be expressed.

***

Lord, bless Ian MacConnacher.[4]
    I hadn't the time
To find a good rhyme
    For such a difficult 'moniker'.

From the start of this new Trades House Year,
    We'll meet challenges face on,
Led by this Mason,
    A Civil, indeed, Engineer.

Thou who hearest all our requests,
    Bless, please, our food, all our crafts, and our guests.

***

[3] Roy Scott, Deacon Convener, surgeon urology department, Glasgow Royal Infirmary, Deacon Convener, 2000–1; ex-Deacon of Incorporation of Tailors.
[4] Ian MacConnacher, Deacon Convener 1999–2000.
Ex-Deacon Incorporation of Masons. Civil engineer.

Deacon Convener's Millennium Dinner

Inevitably, Lord, just a matter of time,
    For 'Millennium' I've looked in vain for a rhyme –
Like MacConnacher hard to fit in the mosaic [5]
    Enough to make anyone just be prosaic.

Among these Conveners are present most 'Exes'
    And only one 'Late', nor yet some from both sexes.
To see them all gathered together in strength,
    If laid end to end they would stretch to some length.
As for years under them by Thee we've been blest,
    In ways some of which we could never have guessd.
So we pray Thee tonight bless us all with Thy grace,
    As through them Thou hast given so much to this place.

***

Once more, O Lord, our year begins.
    We pray that Thou wilt bless
Our guests, our friends, forgive our sins –
    What they are, who may guess?

On our Convener blessings pour.
    A Gardener by the sea,
A CA, and a sailor, more
    One could not wish to be –

Except to lead this House. May we
    As Craftsmen in the past,
For these Thy gifts give thanks to Thee,
    And serve Thee first and last. [6]

***

[5] Ian MacConnacher, Deacon Convener 1999–2000.
Ex-Deacon Incorporation of Masons. Civil engineer
[3] Ian Scott, CA, Deacon Convener 1997-8; ex-Deacon Incorporation of Gardeners. Served RNVR.

Here, as we stand, Lord,
Bless Kenneth Sandford, [7]
The Platform and each Master Court.
Like showers of sand poured
From Thy gracious hand, Lord
Thy blessings to each one be brought.

We can't all be Gardeners,
We pray Thee, Lord pardon us,
May Ken make us work with a will.
Give us more hardiness,
O'ercome our tardiness,
And help him his plans to fulfil.

For the two hundred years,
With more laughter than tears,
The House has enjoyed in this Hall.
For this food which best cheers
Us at one with our peers,
We give Thee our praise, Lord of all.

***

Our forefathers, Lord, were men of compassion,
Though now lovingkindness may seem out of fashion,
Their fellows they cared for when aged or ill,
And helped their dependants their dreams to fulfil.

Now led by a Tailor, we'll keep that tradition,
(Though not one for stitching, he's good at addition),
Like many a Tailor he's quick with accounts,
So bless Thou this food, Lord, in gracious amounts.
Bless David, O Lord, in his 'Year of Dinners', [8]
May this one and all of them be truly winners.

***

---

[7] Kenneth Sandford, Deacon Convener 1994–5, ex-Deacon Incorporation of Gardeners.
Chairman family firm of confectioners. Served RNVR.
[8] David Watson, CA, Deacon Convener 1996–7, ex-Deacon Incorporation of Tailors.

Lord, long ago each different Trade
    With talent and compassion,
Employed their skills and gave their aid
    Our common life to fashion.
Lord, bless our food, each hand and heart,
    That we build well to last;
And with Thy gifts each do his part
    Well worthy of the past.[9]

        ***

We've much to be thankful to Thee for, Lord,
    Although we often moan:
For this House and Craftsmen in accord,
    For Thy gifts of providence outpoured,
And this year, for Sandy Bone. [10]

We always thank Thee before we eat
    In anticipation of a treat,
And expectation of being replete,
    Knowing later we'll have to atone.
But tonight we thank Thee not just for our meat –
    Our thanks, O Lord, for A Bone.

        ***

[9] Deacon Convener Roy A. Johnson, CA, 1990–1; ex-Deacon Incorporation of Cordiners.
[10] Alexander A. H. Bone, Deacon Convener 1993–4, ex-Deacon Incorporation of Wrights Chairman, family steel firm.

Each incorporated Trade
Built on the foundation laid
By Saint Mungo where the Molendinar ran.
We, their sons, who bear their name,
Now perpetuate their fame
With benevolence bestowed where'er we can.

Bakers' bread and Fleshers' meat,
Lord, and everything we eat,
Not to mention drink, are gracious gifts from Thee.
With such blessings in our life
Under Dr Morton Fyfe[11]
We, like children, are as happy as can be.

★★★

INCORPORATION OF BARBERS
Motto: 'In the Presence of God'

The Bible tells of Delilah,
A Philistine bursting with charm.
Samson loved her, but often he'd rile her,
So she vowed that she'd do him harm.

As he slept on her knee she betrayed him,
When he'd said his strength lay in his hair.
With scissors and razor she shaved him,
Bald, and weak as a baby. Beware!

'In the Presence of God' we are meeting.
May that not be an empty boast.
Bless the food which we'll shortly be eating,
And bless Deacon Hogg, Lord, our host.

★★★

[11] Deacon Convener Dr W. Morton Fyfe, 1995–6; (ex-Deacon of Incorporation of Bakers).
Paediatrician.

400TH ANNIVERSARY

Barbers and Surgeons long ago
    Combined to let much bad blood flow,
Believing their kindest cuts could cure
    Such ills as life made folk endure.

King James the Sixth gave them their Charter
    To give close shaves – a royal starter.
As 'In Thy Presence', Lord we pray,
    Bless their four hundredth year today.
Bless, too, this food they with us share,
    And all who make our hair their care.

***

INCORPORATION OF BONNETMAKERS AND DYERS
Motto: 'Give glory to God – Concordia Corroborat.' (Harmony Invigorates)

Thou gavest men, O Lord, to wear
    For ornament a head of hair.
But hair gets thin, and men grow bald
    The weather, too, can get 'gey cauld'.
So craftsmen made, to wear upon it,
    The good Scots cap we call a bonnet.
These Bonnetmakers bless, O Lord,
    And Dyers joined in one accord.
May friendship them invigorate,
    As these Thy gifts in glass, on plate.
Then, as we homeward skip or plod,
    Glory may we give To God.

***

I often wonder, Lord, why a
      Bonnetmaker is also a Dyer.
Perhaps they were two different Trades,
      Who made bonnets in various shades
And is that why we find in their motto,
      Both 'Glory to God' – (Voce Sotto)
And 'Concordia Corroborat',
      Meaning 'Union is Strength' and all that?
Bless friendships formed under the Bonnet.
      Bless our meal. May thy grace rest upon it.

***

ANNUAL DINNER DANCE

This evening, Lord, should have deserved a Sonnet
      In praise of all who ever made a Bonnet
Forgive me, Lord, perhaps another time.
      Meanwhile, I pray, accept this humble rhyme.
Bless Deacon Rob McPhail, Collector Flynn.
      Their kindness surely all our thanks must win.
And bless our food, our friendship – may the dance
      With ladies and their charms our hearts entrance.

***

INCORPORATION OF CORDINERS
Motto: 'God is our Hope'

This craft, whose forebears once made shoes
      With piety and skill,
Be pleased to bless. Their talents use,
      Their cup with gladness fill.

And though among them there be few
      Skilled in their ancient trade,
We pray Thee, 'heal' their hearts anew,
      Their 'souls' on Thee be stayed.

***

INCORPORATION OF GARDENERS

It's hard to believe
    That Adam and Eve
Diggèd and rakèd
    Completely naked!
No doubt, 'twas the flies
    That opened their eyes,
And not just the fruit
    Turned their thoughts to a suit,
To give them protection
    Ere Natural Selection
Had hastened their end.
    All Gardeners defend,
Lord. And in this venue
    Please bless our menu,
Each dish, cold or hot.
    And bless Deacon Scott.[12]

***

---

[12] Ian Scott, CA, Deacon Convener 1997-8; ex-Deacon Incorporation of Gardeners. Served RNVR.

Lord, for Adam it was a wonderful life
 In that garden which was Thy gift;
And when Thou gavest him Eve for his wife
 His heart must have had such a lift.

And when he said, 'Shall we go out tonight?
 She said, not, 'I've nothing to wear!'
But said, 'Yes my dear!' from a heart which was light,
 Though not only her wardrobe was bare.

And every day when the bright sun shone
 She might say, 'What's doing today?'
And Adam would answer, 'We've got nothing on –
 We'll eat, and we'll drink, and we'll play.'

Now, Lord, we come, Gardeners and our wives,
 But Sin has made us conform;
And in contrast with Eden, O Lord, our lives
 Are dull, and toil is the norm.

So bless us, we pray, and these gifts of Thy grace.
 Grant we use them with wisdom and cheer
Lord, be Thou the Unseen Guest in this place,
 In the heart of everyone here.

★★★

INCORPORATION OF HAMMERMEN
Motto 'By Hammer in Hand All Arts do Stand'

(The senior craft of the the Trades House,
though some other crafts have (muted) reservations about this.)

'By Hammer in Hand all Arts do Stand' –
    We welcome each gift as from Thy hand.
The Hammer, the skill, the food, the wine –
    All these are ours. May we be Thine.

          ★★★

There are various crafts this House can boast,
    Such as Tailors, Wrights, and Bakers.
Coopers and Cordiners rate a toast,
    As do Barbers and Bonnetmakers.

Maltmen and Fleshers, each has a claim,
    Gardeners also, and Skinners;
Weavers and Masons may say the same
    At their respective dinners.

But all of these crafts their debt must record
    To one thing which, though it lacks glamour,
Is the gift for which we most praise Thee, Lord,
    With this food and these friends – the Hammer!

          ★★★

Few of us, Lord, are engaged in making
    Things in leather, iron, silver, gold;
Those in shipyards or in engineering
    Could on quite few fingers now be told.
But we ask Thy blessing, Lord, this evening
    On these mercies from Thy gracious hand,
We, the sons of men who used the Hammer,
    That by which alone 'all arts do stand.'

          ★★★

To Hammermen in days of old
    Thou gavest skills to fashion gold,
Silver, iron, tin, and leather,
    Then the will to join together.
We, their sons, around this friendly board,
    Ask Thy blessing, now and ever, Lord.

★★★

O God, who givest us to make
    Utensils with the Hammer –
Ships and machines in yards and shops
    Where all is noise and clamour.
Forgive us – slow to give Thee thanks,
    We hesitate and stammer.
But grace our brotherhood, we pray,
    United by the Hammer.

★★★

We give Thee thanks for all Thy gifts –
    For open Autumn weather,
For those who strike (while the iron's hot),
    Make saddles out of leather;
Who hit the nail right on the head;
    From silver, tin, and gold
Make things of beauty and of use
    Now, as in days of old.
Giver of food, drink, and good cheer,
    Bless Hammermen assembled here.

★★★

Our forebears, Lord, were hard and strong,
    Giants of gentle skill,
Who worked to the beat of the Hammer's song,
    Bent metal to do their will.

At hardship, Lord, they merely laughed.
    With these gifts grant us Thy grace,
To honour the men of this ancient Craft
    Who praised Thee in this place.

           ★★★

Thou knowest every Hammerman, O Lord, would wish to be
    A man involved in building ships proudly to sail the sea;
Or else a Loriner who makes for a horse's mouth the bit,
    And as a Spurrier the spurs, just to encourage it.
Such craftsmen, Lord, of long ago this evening we remember,
    And some who gave their lives in wars, this eleventh of November.
May their great, unseen Brotherhood be with us here tonight,
    And may Thy blessing on our meal us all with them unite.

           ★★★

Lord, as we think of all the Arts
    Which by the Hammer stand,
Let there be none but happy hearts
    With these gifts from Thy hand.

Each heart an anvil where we frame
    Plans for the common good;
And whence we lift praise to Thy Name
    Who givest us our food.

           ★★★

Edward – 'Hammer of the Scots'
     Tied Wallace – and himself – in knots.
Hammers hit nails upon the head;
     We sometimes hit our thumbs instead.

Lord, may all craftsmen's arts still stand
     By hammer held in skilful hand,
Bringing delight and honest gain
     Nor ever causing ill or pain.

As we are blessed with these good gifts,
     His heart with thanks each craftsman lifts.

★★★

The muscled Hammermen of old
     Put rivets in their place;
Or delicately worked in gold
     A filigree of grace.

Lord, bless each Hammermen today
     With strong and skilful hand.
And by these gifts of Thine, we pray,
     May all his arts still stand.

★★★

'The Smith a mighty man is he,'
     We sing, and we would mighty be.
Our brows are 'wet with honest sweat'
     From surfing through the Internet,
Seeking by every skilled transaction
     To give and get our satisfaction.

Blessed are those whom we remember
     On this Eleventh of November.
Bless, Lord, Thy gifts of food and drink.
     May we not speak before we think,
Even if, thanks to Deacon Stirrat,
     There is no lack of the right spirit.

★★★

Each Hammerman should bless the Horse
    Who gave our fathers work,
To make the saddle and, of course,
    Shoes which no ground would shirk.

We who now ride on horse-powered wheels,
    To Thee our glad hearts raise
Thanks for this meal which we all feel
    Merits our boundless praise.

***

'England's on the anvil,' once Kipling wrote with pride,
    'Clanging for the Severn to the Tyne.'
He might have sung of Scotland, especially the Clyde,
    Where Hammermen built ships supremely fine.

And though the shipyard hammers now are silent and so still,
    The spirit of those men lives on today.
We thank Thee for Thy gifts, O Lord, of vision and of skill.
    Bless now our food and fellowship, we pray.

***

INCORPORATION OF TAILORS
Motto: 'Arte Laboratae Vestes' (Clothes Worked with Skill)

Clothes were a sin in the Garden of Eden –
　　Seemed to be things Adam should't be needin'.
But now, Lord, we thank Thee for 'Clothes Worked with Skill',
　　And for this provision – let each eat his fill.
Lord, bless all the Tailors with spiritual riches,
　　That their entertainment may keep us in stitches!

　　　　　★★★

INCORPORATION OF WEAVERS
Motto: 'Weave Trust with Truth'

How many of us in this room
>Are competent to work a loom?
But grant us, Lord, before we leave,
>Lasting friendships here to weave.
Keep us from words and deeds uncouth,
>And with Thy gifts 'Weave Trust With Truth'.

***

O Lord, bless the Weavers.
>We pray Thee, believe us,
We all try to Weave Trust With Truth.
>From Thy heavenly locker
Pour gifts on Bob Stocker –
>Vision, Strength, and the Spirit of Youth.

May the cloth of our life, warp and woof,
>Be with friendship warm, never aloof.
As we work at our loom,
>Be Thou here in this room.
Of Thy love let these gifts be the proof.

***

Bless Lord, we pray, whatever looms,
>All those who use a shuttle.
In sunshine's blaze or shadows' glooms
>Grant them Thy presence subtle.

Whatever cloth of life we weave,
>Cleanse it from stains uncouth.
Bless these Thy gifts which we receive.
>Help us 'Weave Trust with Truth'.

***

Lord, we thank Thee for the Weavers who have never proved deceivers,
    But in friendship, work, and home 'Weave Trust with Truth'.
Help us, gathered round this table, eat and drink as we are able,
    Nor commit, nor suffer, anything uncouth.

Thee with them we celebrate that in 1528
    This Incorporation saw its early days.
Now, we pray Thee, give us grace, as we gather in this place,
    To give Thee, O God, the glory and the praise.

★★★

Lord, though we rarely sit at looms,
    We 'Shuttle' often to these rooms,[13]
Not just to eat but also plan
    New schemes to help our fellowman.
May we with one another 'Weave
    Trust with Truth' that, when we leave,
The fabric of this evening's pleasure
    May remain a joy to treasure.
For these Thy blessings, cold and hot
    We thank Thee, Lord, and Deacon Scott.

★★★

[13] 'Shuttle' was the British Airways Glasgow–London service. Fares were paid in flight and there were no refreshments.

INCORPORATION OF WRIGHTS
Motto: 'Join All in One'

Lord, we thank Thee for the Wright
        Who made for men in wood
The boat to sail, the bow to fight,
        The wheel and so much good.

May we discern Thy guiding hand
        In all we seek to make.
May Christ the Craftsman with us stand.
        Lord, bless us for His sake.

★★★

The glaziers, painters, and sawyers of old,
        The men who made longbow and boat,
Were men who loved fellowship, precious as gold,
        The good of their Craft to promote.
To us the tradition of 'Join All In One'
        They have given, so help us unite,
Enriched with Thy blessing in food, drink, and fun,
        Let us worthily honour The Wright.

★★★

Lord, bless each Wright
        And every guest,
And may tonight
        Our food be blest.
Grant us Thy grace,
        Though undeservin'
Shine with Thy face
        On Deacon Mervyn.[14]

[14] Deacon Mervyn Hamilton died in May 2000, aged 57.
His enthusiasm and laughter live on in our memories.

O Lord, we pray Thee, bless each Wright,
  And every guest met here tonight.
Once Wrights were boatwrights, painters, sawyers;
  Now they're accountants, bankers, lawyers,
Surveyors, Lord, whatever else. So
  Bless them all, and Deacon Kelso. [15]
Yes, bless us here, 'Join All In One',
  Our food, our friendship, and our fun.

★★★

We have the word of King Malcolm the Third,
  That the Wrights, Lord, were founded and firmly grounded
When most of the Trades were not much more than shades.
  Workers in wood who did what they could,
As joiners and sawyers, not bankers and lawyers.
  On this four hundredth birthday,
'Good Wishes,' we all say.
  Bless our food and our friendship, through Christ Thy Son.
May the Wrights and their Deacon soon Join All In One.

★★★

SURPRISE PARTY FOR THE CLERK TO THE TRADES HOUSE,
GORDON R WYLIE WS ON HIS FIFTIETH BIRTHDAY.

Lord we'd all be in the dark
  Were it not for our Clerk,
So we bless Thee for Gordon
  Who acts as a Cordon –
Sanitaire more than Bleu. Life's worry and stir
  He calms with a smile
Which no one can rile.
  Grant him rich blessings on his Jubilee
As we all give thanks for him, Lord to Thee.

★★★

---

[15] Banker, sailor, once youngest now one of the longest-serving Elders in Glasgow Cathedral.

2
Medical and Dental

THE ROYAL COLLEGE OF PHYSICIANS & SURGEONS OF GLASGOW
Motto: 'Conjurat amice – Non Vivere sed Valere Vita.'
(It unites in friendly fashion, not to live but to be vigorous with life)

The Faculty of Physicians and Surgeons of Glasgow, later to become the Royal College was founded in 1599 by Maister Peter Low. He is buried in the Cathedral graveyard where, every year in November or December, after worship in the Cathedral, the Council members of the Royal College process out to their Founder's grave where the President lays a wreath and the Minister offers a short prayer.

The Fellows and Members of the Royal College include many university teachers, and it seeks to maintain high standards of teaching, study and research.

The Royal College celebrated its four hundredth anniversary with a year-long programme of events in 1999 culminating in its birthday celebration on 29 November 1999.

> In friendly fashion let life bind us
> Not to live merely but be strong.
> Bless, Lord, these gifts that Thou may'st find us
> Faithful in friendship all life long.

***

God grant this College,
    Bound now and ever
In friendship and knowledge
    Nothing can sever,
Not to live merely
    But, like their title,
Seek to be really
    Healthy and vital.
God be thanked
    Who gives subsistence
For healthy life
    Not mere existence.
O Lord, four hundred years ago
    Came to our city Peter Low;
Friend of the poor, and of the King,
    To poor, not just the rich, he'd bring
Medical skills and tender feeling –
    Twin forces in the art of healing.

By him the Faculty was founded
    In which his standards were well grounded.
On those who follow him today
    Thy richest blessing, Lord, we pray,
And with their skills Thy wisdom give,
    Till all have health, not merely live.

Upon these gifts before us spread,
    On us, too, Lord, Thy grace release,
That we, like him, as it was said,
    May 'live in mirth and die in peace.'

***

Lord, bless these Presidents,
    Visitors and Residents.
May these Physicians
    Reach wise decisions.
Lord, let the Surgeons see
    That calm, not urgency
Will foster healing
    And better feeling.
So with these healthful gifts of Thine,
    Various foods and choicest wine,
Enrich our friendship as we dine.

**

We thank Thee, Lord, who gavest long ago,
    Compact of wit and wisdom, Peter Low.
Friend of the King, befriender of the poor,
    He never scorned to enter any door.
Grant us Thy blessing here, and on this Royal College
    Spread the infection of his wit and love of knowledge.

**

Thanks be to Thee for this above all wealth,
    Not just to live, but to abound in health.
Bless these, Thy servants, bound to share this treasure,
    United in their work and friends in leisure.
Blest by these gifts, may we to all men show
    The wisdom, grace, and wit of Peter Low.

**

For all Thy blessings as we go,
    For wisdom crowning knowledge,
For worthy Maister Peter Low,
    The Founder of this College;
For constant friends through all life's phases
    We offer Thee our humble praises.

**

Let surgeons wield with skill the knife.
      Physicians diagnose and treat.
To Thee who givest us our life,
      We give our thanks for food to eat.

***

Tonight for Maister Peter Low we thank Thee, Lord,
      And for those here who since his day with one accord
Have sworn Thy gifts to them for others so to give,
      That poor or rich find health in life, not merely live.
For food and friendship, thanks we give to Thee,
      Not just in word, but in sincerity.

***

ROYAL COLLEGE PATRONS' DINNER

Lord, bless our Patrons and their Court,
      Who give protection and support
To our College rooted in standards rigorous,
      Not just to live but to be vigorous,
In work and friendship as we see,
      And in their hospitality.
Lord, bless Thy gifts, our friendship here.
      Accept, we pray, our thanks sincere.

***

MOYNIHAN CHIRURGICAL CLUB DINNER

Lord, who hast made the healing rod to burgeon
      And be a hub
Of friendship, work, and blessing for each surgeon
      Within this Club:
Bless them, their guests, and these, Thy gifts tonight.
      And grant us all that brings good friends delight.

***

Biennial Dinner of the Fellows in Dental Surgery

Lord, we thank Thee for the skills
       With which a well-trained dentist fills
All those cavities he drills …

Physically, or in abstraction,
       Grant us each a good extraction,
From Thy gifts, of satisfaction …

We who suffer facial pain
       Join with those who help it wane
(Though it may come back again …)

Bless, we pray, these Fellows Dental.
       Bless our food – that's fundamental!
And add blessings transcendental!

***

Blest art Thou, Giver of all good
       Tonight, who givest us our food;
And with that gift suppliest teeth
       Fittingly, above, beneath.
For all who past life's summit venture,
       May there be found a fitting denture.
Give us gifts manual and mental,
       All clear in mind, in manner gentle.

***

How fast each year, with heedless pace,
     Creates within one's thinning face
The horror of a dental space.
     Lord, keep these Fellows quick in thought,
To implement each new report,
     That High Street dentists be well taught.
To Thee from whom each blessing flows –
     Bloomfield Report, the CDO's,
Our thanks for these gifts, and for those.

★★★

We turn again to Thee, O Lord,
     From drilling and extraction
And pray this food may us afford
     The utmost satisfaction.

Grant us good fellowship, and speech
     With wit and wisdom laced.
Tonight and always may we each
     Be with Thy presence graced.

★★★

Lord, with this food may we be blessed,
     The talk be good; the wine, each guest,
As warm or cool as may be right.

These Fellows school, Lord, so we might,
     As we may need, above, beneath,
Whene'er we feed enjoy sound teeth!

★★★

Lord, who bringest us to earth
    By the miracle of birth,
A step towards Eternity
    Through the doorway of Maternity:
For those who here with care and skill
    Have served so long and serve Thee still,
We thank Thee who for every need
    Doth soul and mind and body feed.

★★★

3
The Media

The Newspaper Press Fund exists throughout the United Kingdom to relieve distress in any form suffered by those who have worked in the industry. Two fundraising lunches are held in Glasgow each year. A distinguished personality in the press, politics or entertainment is always the principal guest.

NEWSPAPER PRESS FUND LUNCHEON

Lord, our thanks for those with skills,
  Who entertain us, give us thrills,
We thank Thee, too, for those who write,
  Help us relive each game, each fight.

Our thanks for those who write no more,
  No longer play, nor ever score.
Remembering those from whom we've learned,
  May we be blessed by grace unearned.

***

Lord, we give thanks for those who write
  To fill the columns of the Press.
To lives o'ershadowed by distress
  May this our Fund bring friendship's light.
Bless Thou our food with joys convivial;
  Raise thoughts and words above the trivial.

***

Lord, there are times, especially *Sunday Times*,
  When Thou art much less obvious than Andrew Neil.[1]
Forgive our blindness, Lord, and these poor rhymes.
  Bless all for whom this Press Fund works, and bless our meal.

***

[1] Andrew Neil was editor of *The Sunday Times* in 1993.

O Lord, we pray Thee, bless John Birt,[2]
    But if his plans should Scotland hurt,
Thou by Thy grace such fate avert,
    Our spirits raise.
Now bless this food, soup to dessert,
    And Thee we'll praise.

***

If only every writer, Lord, were brighter.
    If only every preacher made things clear.
If only we were wealthy,
    Or could, better still, stay healthy,
We'd have little cause for worry or for fear.

But Thou knowest, Lord, we're mostly poor and needy.
    We become a little less fit every day.
Bless this food to make us stronger
    And to live a little longer.
Bless this Press Fund's beneficiaries, we pray.

***

O Lord, we pray that Thou wilt bless
    All whom we loosely call The Press.
Especially those distressed or ill –
    May this event their hope fulfil.

We also pray, Lord, at this time,
    That Thou, in love and power sublime,
Wilt grant Thy blessing on our Team
    And bring to pass each Scotsman's dream,
By keeping Craig Brown's spirits up,[3]
    Sufficiently to win The Cup.
On Thy gifts here Thy blessing pour,
    That we may serve Thee evermore.

[2] John Birt was Director General of the BBC in 1994. Some of his plans appeared to threaten some aspects of broadcasting in Scotland.
[3] Craig Brown was the coach of the Scottish football team and some international players were present at this lunch with the World Cup in the offing.

BANK OF SCOTLAND PRESS AWARDS LUNCH

Though we depend so much on Banks,
    Rightly to Thee we give our thanks
Who givest life in all its facets,
    Vision to maximise our assets.

For each blessed here with an award,
    For all that they describe, record,
For food and drink before us spread,
    Our thanks to Thee be thought and said.

***

Because, O Lord, among Thy sons and daughters,
    Some heed Thy call to them to be reporters
Or journalists, the chosen prophets of our day,
    For whose predictions, true or false, their readers pay.
We thank Thee for this food, and that in this world's strife
    We bank on Thee – a Friend for Everlasting Life.[4]

***

There will be no award
    For the people, O Lord,
Whose lives or whose views
    Are the basis of news;

Whose joy or distress
    Is food for the Press.

But here as we thank
    Both Thee and the Bank
For this food here today,
    Bless them and bless us, Lord, we pray.

***

[4] 'A friend for life' was a claim made in Bank of Scotland publicity.

We thank Thee, Lord, for some who write
> In newspapers for our delight,
Or else our passions to excite.

Lord, though there may be some surprises
> For those who've won or lost the prizes,
Blessings may come in other guises.

For all Thy gifts, Thee, Lord, we thank,
> And for this food Thee and the Bank.

★★★

IBA (INDEPENDENT BROADCASTING AUTHORITY)
Sir Campbell Fraser, Chairman, Scottish Television

Forgive, we pray, Lord, this preamble
> In thanks and praise for Chairman Campbell.
His work capacity is man-size
> Who led us from before this franchise;[5]
And other boards, Dunlop and BAT,
> (We'll maybe say no more of that.)
Pours BP oil on troubled waters –
> What, Grampian? Well, other quarters.
His optimism's plain to see,
> As a supporter of Dundee.
For him and for this food, O Lord,
> We thank Thee. Grant him rich reward.

★★★

[5] The franchises to each TV company had been recently awarded by the IBA.

Radio Industries Club of Scotland Awards Dinner

Behold us, Lord, a little pensive,
　　　Wondering whom they'll choose.
Life is not a Comprehensive.
　　　Some win. Others lose.

Some tonight will win the prizes,
　　　Some get no award.
But we bless Thee, who supplies us
　　　With these gifts, O Lord.

★★★

O Lord, Thou knowest we read in
　　　The Bible that man at the first
Did no work in the Garden of Eden,
　　　Until for the sin
That his wife got him in,
　　　He was punished with work and was cursed.

Some now think that work is a blessing.
　　　For achievement one gets an award.
Their identity's kept us all guessing –
　　　But deserve it who may,
Bless these gifts, we pray,
　　　And may all our work praise Thee, O Lord.

★★★

Glasgow Herald Bicentenary Dinner 1983

O Thou who first didst make Good News
　　　and heralds to report it,
That Love might win, despite abuse;
　　　that all would find who sought it.

Thou to whom all our news is old,
　　　two hundred years a day.
Accept our thanks for gifts untold,
　　　and bless our food, we pray.

WILLIAM BROWN, CBE, MANAGING DIRECTOR, SCOTTISH TELEVISION
(Retirement Dinner, 31 May 1990)

Lord, ere we start to eat our fill
        of such good things as take our fancy,
We thank Thee for the work of Bill,
        His friendship and, of course, for Nancy.[6]

If changes in that other Bill[7],
        Have left us yet an anxious frown,
Our food and friendship bless, and still
        We'll thank Thee that we've known Bill Brown.

***

BBC GOVERNORS' DINNER, GLASGOW

Lord, in the heavenly country bright,
        May it be just the ticket,
That some may play both day and night
        The matchless game of Cricket.

And even now there some may see
        Thy smile and think it funny,
To see the mighty BBC
        Run out for lack of money.[8]

Bless, Lord, for Thou dost know the score,
        This food for us provided.
To save both Radios Three and Four
        May they by Thee be guided.

***

---

[6] Nancy, Bill's wife, Lady Brown.
[7] Broadcasting Bill, 1990.
[8] The BBC failed to give a high enough financial offer to keep the TV rights for cricket.

O Lord, there's nothing so new about sin;
  No surprise
What people will try in order to win
  A prize.

Lord, Thou knowest what's in every mind.
  We guess
That our own sins are not hard to find.
  But bless
The food Thou hast given tonight,
  And the wine;
And may all that is done here be right
  In our eyes and Thine.

    ***

It's often surprising
  That some advertising
Produces the sales.
  Another just fails.
Thy goodness is hidden
  But here we are bidden
To share in Thy grace.
  And though in the media
Some say, 'We don't need Ya!'
  Lord, keep them a place.

    ***

GLASGOW HERALD DIRECTORS' DINNER

When much of value is imperilled
  We pray Thee for the Glasgow Herald,
That it with truth may wisely lead us.
  Our thanks to Thee who here dost feed us.
    ***

4

I Took My Grace To A Party . . .
but nobody asked me to pray

CONVENER'S RETIREMENT DINNER

We all feel it's dandy
     that Lucille and Sandy[1]
To mark his year
     as Deacon Convener
Have asked us all here.

None could be keener
     Than we here who gather.
Bless Sandy, Lucille
     With happiness, Father,
Our friendship, this meal.
     And when it is done,
Lord, 'Join All In One'[2]
     Our glasses to raise
To them both, and Thee praise.

***

---

[1] Alexander A.H. Bone, Deacon Convener 1993–4, ex-Deacon Incorporation of Wrights. Chairman, family steel firm and his wife Lucille.
[2] 'Join All in One' is the motto of the Incorporation of Wrights.

Bless Ailene, Lord, we pray and Ian[3]
    Whose praise we sing
More than mere song of praise – a Paean,
    As Greeks did bring

To him they called 'The Gods' Physician',
    Who kept them well,
So Ian in his prime position,
    We all can tell

Has kept the House and its funds wealthy,
    As CA's should,
And to ensure that we stay healthy,
    Gave us good food.

Lord, bless them with well-earned retirement,
    At home in Rhu.
To Thee for meeting each requirement,
    Our thanks are due.

★★★

SCOTTISH POLICE FEDERATION JOINT CENTRAL COMMITTEE DINNER

Grant to all who gather here, the riches of Thy grace.
    Bless our friendship with good cheer. Let goodwill fill this place.
Thee who hast Thy children fed in every generation,
    Now we thank, and pray Thee lead and guide this Federation.

[3] Ian Scott, CA, Deacon Convener 1997-8; ex-Deacon Incorporation of Gardeners. Served RNVR.

INCORPORATION OF HAMMERMEN CEILIDHS

(These two Graces are in the rhythm of
well-known Scottish Country Dances.)

As we meet together, Lord, to eat and dance,
      We beseech Thy blessing may Thy gifts enhance,
For we shouldn't want to leave anything to chance
      Ere we dance the hours away.
May Hammermen leave all their work behind,
      Remember to bestow only looks that are kind
On their wives and also on others,
      Fellow-craftsmen and true brothers.
Whatever they work in, be it silver or gold,
      As blacksmiths or tinsmiths or saddlers so bold,
May all crafts stand by the Hammer they hold.
      Bless our food, and bless us, we pray.

***

Ere we say any more
      Or take to the floor
To the beat of the Hammermen's feet,
      Tonight, as of yore
We humbly implore
      Thee to bless us and with us our meat.

Then let time advance
      As we join in the dance
Showing skill with the foot not the hand.
      Please share in our pleasure
As we tread a measure
      By whose Hammer, Lord, all arts do stand.

***

For the arts of the Hammer
    From ships built 'midst clamour
To jewellery's glamour
    We give Thee our thanks.

For the joys of a ceilidh
    Where dancers whirl gaily
For food and drink daily
    We give Thee our thanks.

***

BONNETMAKERS AND DYERS

We pray, Lord, bless our table here,
    The good gifts of Thy love upon it.
Fill every heart with happy cheer,
    As we praise those who made the Bonnet
In serving others may we never tire,
    And so bring honour to the name of Dyer.

***

INSTITUTE OF BANKERS

O God, when funds are running low
    We give Thee hearty thanks
That e'en our small investments grow
    Protected by the Banks.

So bless this Institute, we pray,
    Our fellowship, our food,
And may we use them so that they
    Promote the common good.

***

ROYAL GLASGOW INSTITUTE OF FINE ARTS

Artists express their inspiration
    And fill our hearts with admiration.
With Thy bountiful providing
    Bless us with thy grace and guiding.

***

BANK OF SCOTLAND PRESS AWARDS

Lord, for those by whom is written
    All the news;
News from abroad and news of Britain[4],
    As they choose.
For this food provided, Lord,
    Thee we thank.
And for giving each award,
    Bless the bank.

***

STRATHCLYDE JOINT POLICE BOARD

Bless this food provided, Lord,
    Abundant no parsimony.
Bless the work of this Joint Board,
    And Chairman William Timoney.

***

[4] Reference to pricipal guest, Sir Leon Britten, Home Secretary.

5

Industry & Business

CBI SCOTLAND ANNUAL DINNER

O Lord, since these good things are of Thy giving,
    Help us use them for wiser living;
Each use restraint, reduce inflation,
    To be a slimmer, fitter nation;
And not be sunk in deep depression,
    When waist-, and hair-lines face recession,
O Lord Thou must with interest wait,
    Which one will next devaluate?
Lord, guide us in our problems from on high,
    And for this evening bless the CBI.

        ***

Against the Dollar and the Yen
    The Euro falls, O Lord, again.
Made anxious by the MPC,[1]
    We turn for confidence to Thee.
For Thou canst raise our interest rate
    In Thy good gifts upon each plate.
Contented, then, may we give heed,
    To all the wisdom of John Reid.[2]
Thy richest blessings from on high
    Bestow on Scotland's CBI.

        ***

Thou alone knowest, Lord, what we'll do –
    Join or not join the EMU.
The CBI says, 'Join.' But, Oh,
    The smaller businesses say, 'No.'
Should we have raised the interest rate,
    For fear the economy may inflate?
Lord, bless us here with Currie eating,[3]
    Save us, at least, from overheating.

[1] Monetary Policy Committee which decides interest rates.
[2] John Reid, then Secretary of State for Scotland.
[3] Hugh Currie, President CBI, Scotland.

Lord, while the interest rate stays high,
    Look kindly on the CBI.
And move, we pray, the MPC
    To give some help to industry.
Bless Thou the food, liquid potation,
    And keep us from excess inflation.

***

God knows it's pretty hard to make a living,
    But two things here tonight we must not shirk –
For these good gifts to offer our thanksgiving,
    And know our problems must be solved by work.

***

Faced with the problem of Poll Tax defaulters;
    ERM entry later or right now;
We thank Thee that Thy goodness never alters.
    For these good gifts, our Father, blest be Thou.

***

With science places in short supply,
    May students, O Lord, bless the CBI
For giving a boost to science teaching
    With a scheme perceptive and far-reaching.
And Lord, we welcome Chancellor Clarke.
    Grant he won't put us in the dark,
Or leave the elderly to freeze
    With bills increased by V-A-T's.

May he lower the tax on malts and blended,
    That restraints on our national drink be ended.
Bless, Lord, our food and our friendship here,
    And the dark, after Clarke, be filled with good cheer.[4]

---

[4] This refers to Kenneth Clarke, then Chancellor of the Exchequer.

INSTITUTE OF PETROLEUM, WEST OF SCOTLAND BRANCH

The Institute of Petroleum is a centre of scientific, technical and economic data and expertise for the UK and overseas oil industries. It exists to inform its 7,000 individual and 300 company members about the industry, standards and codes of practice. It has thirteen regional branches.

We give Thee thanks for those who toil
    Here or across the sea;
Whose labours bring to us the oil
    Which we all owe to Thee.

And though we come from different lands,
    Have different faiths as well,
With BP, Chevron, we join hands,
    With Texaco and Shell.

Please bless our food and friendship, Lord,
    Even now before we've eaten.
With one accord around this board,
    Let us all thank Bill Beaton[3]

***

O hear us, Lord, ere we have eaten:
    We thank Thee for our host, Bill Beaton.
For this Institute whose branch he chairs.
    Each year they drive away our cares
With food and drink on lavish scale.
    Lord, may their oil wells never fail.
But Friendship is their greatest pleasure,
    A gift their motto seems to treasure –
'Conjunctione potiores' –
    Wise words which underpin our mores,
Could mean, 'More capable in marriage,
    A boast let none of us disparage.
Or simply, 'Happier in Union.'
    Lord, be with us in our communion.

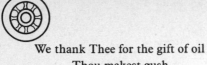

We thank Thee for the gift of oil
    Thou makest gush
From hidden depths beneath the soil
    And sea to rush.

Bless all who profit from its sale
    Counting each share.
Lord, let its rich flow never fail.
    Then might they spare
Some blessings on us here who dine?
    But, Lord, let all the praise be Thine.

              ***

'Conjunctione Potiores' is the motto
    Of this Institute whose guests we are tonight.
So while we're not quite blotto,
    And with 'voce' fairly 'sotto',
Lord, we pray that Thou wilt kindly keep us right.

Lord, this Institute's bold motto is exciting.
    Let each single man, or company, take heed:
'We're more able by uniting' –
    Fewer reasons left for fighting? –
No, the strength of union helps meet every need.

There are spirits which unite quite well with water;
    But, Lord, Benzine's not according to our taste.
So we may be all the merrier
    If we're canny with the Perrier.[6]
Bless our food and drink, Lord, here with Friendship laced.

              ***

---

[6] At the time there was a short-lived scare about Perrier mineral water being tainted with traces of benzene.

The Midnight Hour, Lord, keeps us from our beds,
    And even souls still left at Number Ten,
Where Bernard Ingham once spun thoughtful threads,[7]
    Which Margaret Thatcher wove so finely then.

On troubled waters may Thine oil be poured,
    And in our words as well as oil some wine.
May we feast richly on this food, O Lord,
    And for these gifts let all the praise be Thine.

***

WEST OF SCOTLAND ENGINEERS' ASSOCIATION ANNUAL DINNER

This association, formerly West of Scotland Foremen Engineers Association, united middle management staff from shipyards and other industrial firms.

Lord, for blessings small or greater
    Through the Engineer;
Thou who as the world's Creator
    Art their Pioneer:
With these mercies here provided
    May our lives by Thee be guided.

***

For all Thy guidance, Lord, throughout the years
    Towards the West of Scotland Engineers,
We thank Thee now, and pray that by Thy grace,
    We all may know Thy blessing in this place.

***

O God, who givest man the skill to be an engineer;
    And who in friendship dost unite all who are gathered here:
We thank Thee for this food and drink, for all that cheers the heart;
    And pray that we may please Thee well, who our Creator art.

***

[7] Bernard Ingham, former press secretary to Margaret Thatcher, was the guest speaker.

We thank Thee, Lord, for all who made
    Our engines and our ships;
For all who great traditions laid,
    Put 'Clyde-built' on all lips.
Now grant Thy blessing, Lord, we pray,
    On gifts Thou dost provide.
Through storms and shoals pilot our way...
    Let Thy truth be our guide.

***

CENTENARY LUNCH OF HADEN MACLENNAN
(now Haden Young Ltd., construction engineers.)

We thank Thee, Lord, for Haden MacLellan,
    Amazing the range of things they've been sellin',
From stations and bridges, churches and trains,
    To pontoons and landing craft, pipelines and planes.
Bless them Lord, we pray, on this their centenary
    Who over the years have enhanced so much scenery.
Bless these Thy good gifts, Lord, and help us to see
    That all our achievements are gifts sent from Thee.

***

SCOTTISH MANAGEMENT GROUP
Retirement dinner of Sir Patrick Thomas, Chairman.

Sir Patrick was the former managing director of Beardmores Ltd, Shettleston, an Ex-Deacon Convener of the Trades of Glasgow and a Lt Col in the Royal Armoured Corps. The Scottish Management Group had all forms of transport in Scotland under its control.

O God, we thank Thee for Sir Pat,
    And for this dinner which we're at;
(Or, more correctly, Pat, our friend,
    And this event which we attend!)
For gifts to him he shared with us,
    Managing ferry, boat and bus,
And long before, on hills of knowledge,
    Starting at first in Clifton College,
Cambridge, Africa, Italy, Greece,
    Leader in war, alike in peace;
Hammerman, Deacon, Deacon Convener,
    None more effective, no one keener.

Lord, for these gifts before us spread,
    For this Thy servant, thanks be said.
In work, faith, friendship, Lord, may we,
    Like him, accord our thanks to Thee.

***

SCOTTISH WHOLESALE LICENSED TRADE DINNER

Right from the first,
    Just stop and think,
That God who gives all of us a thirst
    Gives each of us his chosen drink!

Lord, give us tonight both ample measure,
    And sense too, not to spoil folks' pleasure.

★★★

TENNENT CALEDONIAN LIMITED
Tennent's Lager Centenary Luncheon.

O Lord, whose gifts oft bring delight with danger,
    The comfort of a friend, the challenge of a stranger:
May we well use those brewed by TCB,
    And wish their product well upon its century.
Bless the Cathedral's oldest of near neighbours.
    Help us get pleasure only, from their labours.

★★★

MACALASTER & ALISON CENTENARY
(Quoted by Jack House in his centenary history of the company.)

O Thou whose love dost offer
    All eternal life protection:
Accept the thanks we proffer
    For Thy hundred years' direction.
Thus by Thy gracious blessing,
    Macalaster & Alison
Have saved investors guessing,
    And suffering curse or malison.[8]
Lord, grant us at this celebration
    The best of Thy Risk Separation.
Let Fire, Flood, Theft, and Acts of Thine
    Not cloud our pleasures as we dine.

---

[8] Malison is an archaic word for curse.

All the launches and the subsequent lunches took place at the one yard at Scotstoun, originally Yarrows, then GEC Marconi Marine, now BAE Systems. Popularly it is still called Yarrows.

Marconi Marine, May 1999
Launch of HMS *Portland*

O Lord, accept our thanks, we pray,
    For all the blessings of this day –
The ship, the launch, convenient tide,
    This food and drink Thou dost provide.
While Portland, by the Chesil Bank,
    Thee, for their ship, will also thank.
Grant further orders to Marconi,
    We pray Thee, have a word with Tony.[9]

***

Launch of HMS *Kent*
Yarrows GEC, May 1998

We thank Thee, Lord that men of Kent,
    And Kentish men, that name have lent
To ships of old, and new today
    Their Princess speeds her on her way.
To bear that name she is the latest.
    To us she will remain the greatest.
Bless, Lord, the ship and all who've worked
    To build her well, for none has shirked.
Bless Yarrow's. May they get more orders
    To build more ships within their borders.
Bless these Thy gifts, our friendships too.
    We give Thee thanks as is most due.

***

[9] Prime Minister Tony Blair.

Launch of HMS *Monmouth*

We thank Thee. From the land of Gwent
  The name of Monmouth Thou hast lent
To ships of old, and now today.
  Bless all who've worked on her, we pray.
Bless Yarrow's, that they get more orders
  To build more ships within our borders.
For these Thy gifts, our friendships too,
  We give Thee thanks, as is most due.

★★★

Launch of HMS *St Albans*

We've prayed that Thou wilt bless O Lord,
  The last Type 23,[10]
The ship and all who sail in her
  When she puts out to sea.

Saint Alban Thou didst call to be,
  Lord, the first English Saint.
The other ships which bore his name,
  To us seem rather quaint.

Please bless our food, O Lord, and lend
  Thy grace to bless us too.
And many other orders, send
  To Scotstoun not a few.

★★★

[10] Type 23 Frigate, now discontinued.

CIVIC LUNCH FOR THE SHIP'S COMPANY OF HMS GLASGOW

Lord, let Glasgow –
    Both ship and city –
Flourish. As Mungo
    Prayed for Thy pity,
Grant us Thy grace,
    With these gifts Thy blessing,
Each in our place
    In Thy Service progressing.

★★★

OPENING OF THE HOLIDAY INN, GLASGOW
By HRH The Princess Margaret, Countess of Snowdon

A holiday was Thy gift to man
    with the very first day of rest;
But when Christ was born man found no room
    in the inn for the Royal Guest.
Lord, here in Glasgow's Holiday Inn,[11]
    bless our food and our friends, we pray.
And be Thou the unseen Guest to guide
    the staff and the guests each day.

★★★

[11] The Holiday Inn is now called the Marriott.

6
Banking

TRUSTEE SAVINGS BANK

Lord of all life, we humbly thank
    Thee for the Trustee Savings Bank.
Thou hast been saving for so long.
    We, mere beginners, get it wrong.
Help us, like Thee, to save by giving,
    Which is the secret of real living.
Bless to us these gifts of grace.
    Give us in Thy plan a place.

***

Lord, despite our varied cravings,
    Thou wouldst keep us as Thy savings.
By Thy love in Christ revealed
    May we give Thee highest yield.
Grant us, gathered in this place,
    With these mercies Saving Grace.

***

WEST OF SCOTLAND TRUSTEE SAVINGS BANK ANNUAL LUNCH

God, who givest every gift
    Good and perfect, such as Thrift:
Forbid that we should fail to thank
    The West of Scotland Trustee Bank;
And Thee, the Giver of all good,
    For Christmas, Friendship and our food.
While each one here loves to say, 'Yes,'
    Keep us, Lord, from all excess. [1]

***

[1] The Annual Meeting was always just before Christmas.
They had a slogan, 'The bank that likes to say "Yes!". '

TSB
Retirement dinner for Richard Ellis, Chairman, Scotland

Lord, we give Thee thanks tonight for Richard Ellis,
     Scottish Chairman and a member of Group Board.
That he's held in high esteem, Lord, Thou canst tell is
     An opinion we all share with one accord.

Bless, we pray, these good things set upon our table.
     Thanks to Thee, first, for all these, and to the Board.
Bless our friend both good and able,
     Pensions rising, markets stable
Give to each Thy saving grace, good Lord.

★★★

BRITISH LINEN BANK BICENTENARY
To raise funds for the Princess Royal Trust for Carers in the presence of
Her Royal Highness, The Princess Royal

Bless, Lord, The Princess Royal Trust
    for Carers; and we thank
for all their kindness, as we must,
    The British Linen Bank.

From credit to the Linen trade
    two-fifty years ago,
expansions, growth, and mergers made
    the Merchant Bank we know.

With them, Lord, blessed may we be
    in this historic venue,[2]
with friendship and these gifts from Thee
    which grace this splendid menu.

***

[2] Palace of Holyroodhouse.

7
Law and Accountancy

INSTITUTE OF CHARTERED ACCOUNTANTS OF SCOTLAND
(This was the first rhyming grace written by me.)

Lord, as the 'freeze' begins to bite
  And economic rigours,
We thank Thee for CA's who read,
  And understand the figures.

Lord, Bless this Institute, we pray,
  And by Thy grace direct
Their lives and ours, that Thou may'st find
  All our accounts correct.

★★★

Bless, O Lord, the food and wine,
  And grant that, as Thy servants dine,
Each appetite, when Thou has fed it,
  May leave a balance to their credit.

★★★

Lord, we thank Thee for the blessings of this dinner,
  For our food, and for the drink, and for our friends;
And although, by all accounts, we won't be thinner,
  We beseech Thy grace that we may make amends.
May the speeches show us wisdom's many facets.
  Grant that brevity may be the soul of wit.
Keep our minds off our depreciating assets.
  May our thanks to Thee ne'er be in deficit.

★★★

ROYAL FACULTY OF PROCURATORS, GLASGOW

Procurator is an ancient legal term, literally meaning one who acts for another person. In mediaeval times the legal agents were based in the consistory courts held in cathedrals such as existed in Glasgow Cathedral. One of the western towers, demolished in mid-19th century was the Consistory House. The Faculty Hall in what is now Nelson Mandela Place, formerly St George's Place, houses one of the finest legal libraries in the country. The Dean and members, with the Sheriff Principal and Sheriffs attend a morning service in the Cathedral every three years when a new Dean assumes office.

CIVIC DINNER, 1996

Lord, as here we celebrate
    The name of Procurator,
Not for us to speculate
    About such nomenclature.

But we know it's false to state
    That some of them still procurate
Or, as solicitors, solicit,
    Such a thing would be illicit.

On their work and skills progressing
    Grant, O Lord, we pray, Thy blessing.
For our food and friendship, we
    Offer heartfelt thanks to Thee.

***

BICENTENARY BALL, 1996

O Lord, we give Thee thanks tonight
    For the Dean – for Campbell White –
For tending the machinery
    Which drives this Bicentenary.

And, Lord, Thou wilt see that all
    Assembled here will have a Ball;
Those who watch and those who dance
    Feel the magic of romance.

For these gifts we bless Thee, Lord,
    Praise Thy Name with one accord.
With soup, fish, meat, veg, and 'potaters'
    Satisfy these Procurators.

***

Lord, a Procurator's wife
    Must have an awful life,
If she's always found the Law
    Nothing much more than a bore.
'Let all thought of a conveyance
    Be tonight held in abeyance,'
She says. For she'd much rather,
    On an evening like this, gather
With us all to have a feast
    She's not had to make, at least.
So, Lord, bless our food tonight.
    Pray it may bring great delight
To us all here in The Marriott.
    Bless the drink, Lord. Help us carry it …

***

If all folks were flawless
     The world could be lawless.
Though too much enjoyment
     Might still give employment
To lawyers who'd see
     That none should go free
Unless they'd conform
     To some sort of norm.
Or Original Sin would stick its oar in.
     Thanks for Thy gifts in abundant variety.
Help us enjoy them – Of course, with propriety.

★★★

Lest for these gifts of Thy conveyance
     Our duty, Lord, seem in abeyance,
We now declare our thanks to Thee,
     And pray Thee, Bless this Faculty,
The Dean, and all who care on our behalf –
'Procuratores nobis' – and their staff.

★★★

TRIENNIAL DINNER 1980

For those who see to our affairs,
     Procurators in this place;
For these gifts of Thine, and theirs,
     We thank Thee with this heartfelt Grace.

★★★

TRIENNIAL DINNER 1983

Thy laws help us to grow to selfless love.
     In Thee, Lord, Justice and kind mercy meet.
Grant us some foretaste here of joys above.
     Bless, Lord, our friendships, and the food we eat.

★★★

7
Sport

PHOENIX ANGLING CLUB

If I were a fish, a maggot would be
     Just the sort of a dish I would like for my tea.
I think I would squirm if offered a worm,
     And though it's attractive, exceedingly active,
A 'minnow' is cheating – it's unfit for eating!
     Lord, thanks for each dish, that none hides a hook.
May we all, and our fish, find a place in thy book.

***

COMMONWEALTH GAMES FUNDRAISING APPEAL

The Commonwealth Games need people to run
     And jump and throw and walk.
But we, our outstanding feats are done
     More with a knife and fork.

Lord, ere we eat, we offer Thee thanks
     For these blessings on our table.
May we with the help of our friendly Banks
     Give as much as we are able.

So may the Games see Scotland's team
     Attain the triumphs of which we dream.

***

DINNER TO CELEBRATE THE GRANTING OF THE
FREEDOM OF THE CITY OF GLASGOW TO SIR ALEX FERGUSON.

O Lord, it must be a terrible pity
    To be a supporter of Manchester City.
So much success has been won by United,
    Crowned by the manager, Lord, being knighted.

What blessings, Lord, canst Thou still have in store
    For our city's new Freeman? Let them come by the score.
And bless us, we pray, Lord, our food and our wine.
    Let Thy Spirit of friendship bless us as we dine.

***

8
Schools and Education

THE GLASGOW ACADEMY, GOVERNORS' PRIZEGIVING LUNCH
'Serva Fidem' – 'Keep Faith' is the Glasgow Academy motto.

Thee, Lord, we thank for all our joys.
    And, just as much as for the boys,
For those who serve and feed 'em
    Seen in their culinary ploys
Thy benediction never cloys,
    Thy gifts come as we need 'em.

***

We thank Thee for these gifts of grace,
    Our bodies feel they need 'em.
But our souls too must have their place.
    Help us 'Servare Fidem.'

***

Lord, all these blessings of Thy grace
    Are welcome and we heed 'em.
We thank Thee. Help us in this place
    Always 'Servare Fidem.'

***

We thank Thee for the motto 'Serva Fidem',
    Thus calling us, O Lord, to Keep the Faith.
Look on Thy servants, Lord, and richly feed 'em
    So save each one from looking like a wraith.
Lord, with Thy gifts, bless every Academical,
    And with Thy peace drive out all thoughts polemical.

***

We thank Thee for the food we eat,
    O Lord, and also Mrs Peat,[1]
Her staff who cook and serve and feed 'em,
    Here for the hungry when they need 'em.
Bless these Thy gifts, each one a prize
    From Thee who all good things supplies.

***

RETIREMENT PARTY FOR COLIN TURNER, RECTOR

O Lord, who lovest all Thy creatures
    And even each poor learner,
In Thy benevolence gave teachers,
    Among them Colin Turner.

For almost twelve years we've been blest
    By his wise, kindly guiding.
So much achieved, but who'd have guessed
    He'd leave an' no' be biding.

Lord, for the friendship he has brought us
    For all the lessons he has taught us,
We give Thee thanks and praise.
On him, Priscilla, sons and daughters,
    Pour out Thy grace always.

***

[1] Mrs Peat is the Catering Officer.

GLASGOW ACADEMICALS' CLUB DINNER

O Lord, who givest all some talents,
    But more than most to Ian Vallance,[2]
Leaving the rest of us a balance:
    To this Academy we're bound,
With cords of friendship, round and round.
    May we within Thy grace be found.
A hundred years have passed, and fifty,
    Studded with stars, their footwork nifty,
Or quick of brain, their outlook thrifty.
    Thou lovest all, both saint and sinner.
Prosper our outer man, and inner,
    And grant Thy blessing on our dinner.

★★★

Lord, as we end another year,
    And take a fond farewell,
Let us give thanks for Thy gifts here,
    Keep Faith with friends both far and near,
Keep Faith in Thee as well.

★★★

[2] Ian Vallance, British Telecom Chief Executive, and a Glasgow Academical.

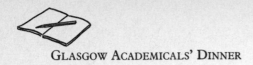

GLASGOW ACADEMICALS' DINNER

When we first came to Colebrooke Street
    With not a girl in sight,
We came, O Lord, with dancing feet,
    And every heart was light.

Then Lachie taught us all the drill
    McGregor made work fun.
Miss Teggart soothed our every ill,
    And all our games were won.[3]

At least, that's how it seems, O Lord,
    As we recall those days.
`Bless these Thy gifts, this well-filled board,
    And Thine be all the praise.

***

UNIVERSITY OF STRATHCLYDE SUPPER & CONCERT

If music be the food of love indeed,
    Give us tonight at least sufficient
That we elsewhere may be efficient.
    And may the music of Thy love us feed.

***

---

[3] Lachlan Robertson and Ian McGregor, two popular teachers and Rachel Teggart, secretary

When the Romans, Lord, came to these islands,
    They looked in vain for a guide.
It was even worse in the Highlands
    Where the natives could easily hide.

So Scotland they called, 'Caledonia' –
    'The Land of the People who Hide.'
But the climate gave Romans pneumonia,
    And here their ambitions just died.

But the Greek Celedones – the 'Charmers',
    Were a song-group of mythical girls,
Like the sirens, but perfectly harmless,
    Who delighted the lads with their twirls.

Gladden us with our third university.
    May its work 'For the Common Weal'
Help us all to conquer adversity.
    And so we thank Thee for this meal.

***

O Lord, bless every graduate
    And every guest.
So may we all be glad we ate
    A meal so blest.

Of Thy great mercy, bless this place.
    And bless each seat
Of learning elsewhere. By Thy grace
    Bless now our meat.

        ***

Almighty and most gracious God:
    The hour swiftly on us looms
When as our Chancellor Lord Tooms
    Will take the place graced by Lord Todd.

We thank Thee, Lord, for every gift
    Which Thou hast given to Strathclyde;
And for this food Thou dost provide
    Our grateful hearts to Thee we lift.

        ***

    There is only one among us who can dance an entre-chat
One makes books and TV programmes sent to viewers near and far;
    Only one can make a sculpture of his friends – completely stoned;
One paints pictures which his friends show, sold, we hope, not merely loaned;
    For all these, we thank Thee, Father; for our Chancellor, Lord Todd.
For his twenty-five years guidance we give praise to Thee, O God.
    And although quite undeserving of the good things on our plate,
We'll give thanks to Thee and feel 'Honoris Causa' glad we ate.

        ***

OUTWARD BOUND DINNER

Lord, Who Thyself art outward bound
    Always beyond our farthest sight
Yet near, wherever need is found,
    In our souls' darkness giving light.

Bless those who, having heights achieved,
    Help others test and stretch their skill.
With these good things we have received,
    Give us an undefeated will.

Bless Outward Bound, concerned with others,
    Not sparing themselves, helping their brothers,
Giving youth vision, helping them feel
    Transformed by their time spent at Loch Eil.
Bless this our food, and grant that we
    Forget ourselves in serving Thee.

***

HUTCHESON'S GRAMMAR SCHOOL
Retirement dinner for David Ward, Rector

For David Ward
    We thank Thee, Lord.
'Truth', the motto of this school,[1]
    He embodies, truly 'cool'.

Came here, then a man of mystery,
    Had taught and written, here made, History.

Greater now the School he leaves.
    At his going our heart grieves.
Bless our meal. But we, possessed
    Of his achievements are most blest.

[1] Veritas

9
Robert Burns

GRACES FOR BURNS SUPPERS

Some hae meat they canna eat
      Haggis, for example.
But we can eat it – it's a treat.
      A little isnae ample.
For daily bread and nightly bed,
      With an electric blanket;
For sangs and words, when wisely said,
      Thy Name, O Lord, be thankit.

★★★

O Thou that in the heavens dwells
      And gies us each guid gift.
The giftie gie tae see oorsels
      An' needy neebors lift.

For some hae meat and canna eat,
      E'en here within this City.
But we hae meat an' we can eat,
      On them, Lord, show Thy pity.

The warld we ken has mony turns.
      Some hae nae meat that want it.
By helping them we'd honour Burns,
      An sae, Thee, Lord, be thankit.

★★★

'Some hae meat and canna eat'
  Even in Strathclyde Region.
'But we hae meat, and we can eat.'
  Those like us, Lord, are legion.
'The world,' we know, 'has many turns,'
  'Some hae nae meat that want it.'
Let us help them and honour Burns,
  'And sae the Lord be thankit.'

10
Clubs, Societies, Associations & Trusts

THE BORDERS CLINICAL CLUB ANNUAL DINNER

For this Borders Club most clinical
May this evening be the pinnacle
    Of a happy year.
They, skilled in the art of healing,
We, their friends, with no ill-feeling
    Seek Thy blessing here.

May Thy providence be dealing
Food and drink, rich gifts revealing
    Of the chef's rare arts.
And Thy goodness in large doses
Soon confirm the best prognosis
    Of our hopeful hearts.

***

Professionally we're clinical.
    Effect to cause we trace,
But we are not too cynical
    To recognise Thy grace.
We thank Thee for this food our bodies need.
    Our minds and souls as well, we pray Thee, feed.

***

BRITISH SAILORS' SOCIETY BRITANNIA BALL

For many years the British Sailors Society had a Scottish Committee, an office in Bath Street, hostels with managerial staff, a Scottish Chaplain, a number of honorary Port Chaplains, a home at Rhu, Dunbartonshire, for the children of seafarers, the Sir Gabriel Wood Home, Greenock, a sheltered housing complex for retired seafarers and their wives, a number of ladies' fundraising guilds across Scotland, a garden fête at Rhu in the summer, and in the winter a Britannia Ball preceded by a dinner in a hotel in Glasgow. This was one of the highlights of the winter social season for many people. For so many people, changing circumstances and economies resulted in much of this work coming to an end and many voluntary workers lost their motivation and inspiration as a consequence.

> O Lord, we thank Thee for our food and drink.
> We say these words of Grace with careless ease.
> Give us the sense more gratefully to think
> Of those who for our good sail many seas.
> And may their children by our gifts, though small
> Share in the joy of this Britannia Ball.

***

> Be near, we pray, this and every day
> To those who are all at sea.
> Their children too, in the Home at Rhu
> We now commend to Thee.
> Give everything good at Sir Gabriel Wood
> To the sailors home from the sea,
> And may we all by means of this Ball
> Bless them and give glory to Thee.

***

> For those who sail upon the sea,
> Father, we give thanks to Thee.
> With food and friends and all
> Be present. Help us have a Ball.

***

They used to blow a horn of gold
    In the year of Jubilee,
To make sure everyone was told
    They were restored and free.

Restore us, Lord, and make us bold,
    By these good things from Thee,
To dream of architects cajoled
    To work without a fee!

★★★

Once Venice held the gorgeous East
    (Or so we're told!) in fee.
But as we gather at this feast
Venice is sinking, but increased
Are architects and, not the least,
    Our hosts in Jubilee.

May they, like Hebrew slaves of old
    Be both restored and free!
Without a ram's horn of pure gold
By us may all Thy love be told,
As for these good gifts, hot and cold,
    We offer thanks to Thee.

★★★

GLASGOW SHIPOWNERS AND SHIPBROKERS'
BENEVOLENT ASSOCIATION DINNER

Bless, Lord, Shipbrokers and Ship owners,
    May all their dealings yield a bonus
Which they can share in benefactions
    As thanks to Thee for their transactions.
Bless all who are engaged in shipping,
    Their staffs, their clients. Eating, sipping
The good things offered in this dinner –
    Make it for all of us a winner.

★★★

O Lord, Thou hast told us that Jonah
    Brought the crew of a ship rotten luck.
So to save both the ship and her owner,
    To the waves they had Jonah to chuck.
Grant that Shipbrokers now, and Shipowners
    May meet need with generous care.
To this meal add Thy grace as a bonus
    To the friendship which here we all share.

★★★

PLANT OWNERS' ASSOCIATION DINNER

To Thee are known, Lord, those who own
    Equipment for compaction;
And JCB's and things like these,
    Earth moving, rock extraction.

Thee may it please to bless all these
    Who gather here tonight.
Conditions of hire – may they inspire
    Plant Owners to do right.

Circular saws obey Thy laws,
    And every excavator.
When hunger gnaws we turn, of course,
    To Thee, supreme Creator.

Bless then Thy gifts as each heart lifts
    In rich anticipation.
And freed from rifts, unseemly shifts,
    Bless this Association.

***

MASONIC DINNER

Thou knowest, Lord, that Shakespeare
    wrote or sang of old
Of bees – 'the singing masons
    building roofs of gold.'
Bless, then, O Lord, our evening,
    our food be sweet as honey;
The conversation sparkling,
    the speeches short, jokes funny.
May guests and masons be like bees
    and build our lives Thee, Lord, to please.

***

SAINTS & SINNERS CLUB OF GLASGOW

Lord, though we pretend to what we ain't,
    We thank Thee for this dinner;
And pray to make of each a saint
    Who knows himself a sinner.

For saints and sinners are true brothers
    Who serve Thee best in serving others.

★★★

THE NOMADS' CLUB

Behold us, Lord, among the ranks
    Of Nomads – 'wanderers who seek grazing'.
For asking us we give them thanks.
    For food? It's Thee we must be praising.

★★★

These two evening clubs meet for dinner (sometimes), a talk by a member or visitor, and lively discussion (always). They contribute generously to charitable causes.

The North Parish extended from the High Street past the old site of Glasgow University, encompassing the ground eventually to be occupied by Duke Street Prison, the Necropolis, the Royal Infirmary up to Petershill, Cowlairs, and Hamilton Hill. The owners of land to the north and west of the Molendinar Burn, which flows now mainly underground beneath Wishart Street and Duke Street to the Clyde, decided to equip and manage washing-greens on ground to the north-east of the Cathedral. Not only were the conditions for washing of clothes safe-guarded and controlled, but the welfare of the women and the education of their children was undertaken with the support of the Town Council, the Trades House, the Merchants' House, the Chamber of Commerce and the University. The Society continues its charitable work to this day.

> Where once winds blew and washing dried
>   Our fathers took great care,
> Whatever ills might there betide,
> Some help and comfort to provide
>   As much as they could spare.
>
> And though the Molendinar's hid,
>   It flows beneath the ground.
> Grant us Thy blessing, Lord, and bid
> Us do as then our fathers did,
>   Wherever need is found

***

National Hairdressers' Federation Banquet & Ball

Lord, it really seems unfair
That men start to lose their hair
Though they're still quite spry and well within their prime.
Neither liniments nor pills,
Nor this Federation's skills
Can restore these ghastly ravages of time.

But we thank Thee that the girls,
With straight hair or waves or curls
Can delight our hearts and lift our load of care.
Bless, we pray, these gifts of Thine
And our friendships as we dine.
Thanks to Thee from Whom hath come the gift of Hair.

***

The Welding & Joining Society

When our grandfathers wanted strong ships that held,
They'd build them with rivets, and never weld.
But composite metals and lasers today
Have brought us new visions but we'll have to pay.
Ceramics and metals for aerospace rockets
Make Chancellors wince, but empty our pockets.

Lord bless this Institute, guiding research.
Heaven knows mysteries hid from the Church.
With food, drink, and friendship may we be blest,
And find in the speeches wise thoughts to digest.

***

In an H – A – Z,
　　By welders it is said,
When two metals meet
　　The correct pre-heat
Will prevent any metal from cracking.

In this 'Heat-Affected Zone'
　　Let Thy presence set the tone.
Bless us, Lord, in this place,
　　And our food, by Thy grace,
That nothing from our friendship may be lacking.

***

Bless, Lord, our food, for Thou dost give it,
　　This place where this event is held,
Our fathers Thou didst teach to rivet
　　And us, their sons, to join and weld.

So may the speakers rivet our attention
　　With wit and wisdom may we all be held;
And one more thing I must not fail to mention,
　　Join us together. Us in friendship weld.[1]

***

---

[1] I am very grateful to Professor T. Neville Baker, PhD, DMet, DSc, in the Department of Mechanical Engineering, University of Strathclyde for his invaluable assistance with metallurgical terminology. My grandfather, a riveter, had no time for, or faith in, welding.

O Lord our God, Thou hast beheld
    Thy servants here, who sometimes weld,
And now are joining in this function
    On which we ask Thy gracious unction.

May their homogenous components
    Be fused as heated zone exponents,
And weld a structure, free from flaws,
    Of friendship faithful to Thy laws.

Help them avoid lamellar tearing,
    That they together may be sharing
Good food, fine speeches only lacking
    All kinds of fission save wise-cracking.

Like silver alloy, freshly coined,
    May we be, to Thy glory, joined.

***

It used to be that, if one wished to build,
    One had to satisfy the Dean of Guild.
But had the Lord Dean been himself a builder
    Whom he'd have had to please might well bewilder.

For Morrison[2] we thank Thee, Lord –
    A man of many parts:
A host to many at his board;
Leading this house in rich accord;
    Blends business with the Arts.
For him, and for these gifts of Thine,
We thank Thee. Bless us as we dine.

***

Lord, we give Thee thanks for Bonar,[3]
    Kind, respected Dean of Guild.
Praise we bring to Thee, and honour,
    Without whom we vainly build.
Lord, long reverenced in this place,
    Endow these blessings with Thy Grace.

***

[2] Morrison Dunbar, himself a builder by trade.
[3] Bonar Hardie

Even in weather cold and wintry
      There's always warmth and light in Fintry,
Where lives (at least is sometimes seen)
      Our honoured and well-loved Lord Dean;
Descended from Strathclyde of old,
      'Son of the Britons' we are told.

Rich in his friendship, fun and faith
      We thank Thee for Lord Dean Galbraith.[4]
Bless these Thy gifts. We, each his guest,
      Are by his friendship really blest.

★★★

We thank Thee, Lord, for Forbes Macpherson,[5]
      An interesting, well-loved person;
For Margaret too, his charming wife,
      Who shares his busy public life.

For his two years as Dean of Guild
      With duties, as with dinners, filled:
Meeting less often with his liners
      Than with a host of fellow-diners.

In far-off years served in the Navy,
      His gold ring permanently wavy.
Then, later on in SIE,
      The GDA, and TSB...

We, among his honoured friends,
      Thank them both as his term ends;
And pray that Thou this food wilt bless,
      And fill their hearts with happiness.

★★★

[4] David Galbraith
[5] Forbes Macpherson

David has well and truly filled [6]
    The Office of Lord Dean of Guild.
Nor could a city wish for finer
    Devotion that shown by him and Ina.

He, long since risen through the ranks,
    Became a head man in the banks;
A Fellow of their Institute,
    He fears no Ecu substitute.

Burning with zeal for education,
    And interested in Cremation,
A Gardener and a golfer too,
    Keeps to the fairway straight and true.

With thanks to Thee our hearts are filled.
    Bless these Thy gifts and our Dean of Guild.

***

The Grand Antiquity Society of Glasgow

Lord, here with true propriety
    We give Thee thanks for this Society,
Founded in 1756
    For free-born, built in with the bricks;
Chartered in 1899.
    Thus we are privileged to dine,
With thoughts of Grand Antiquity.
    Preserve us from iniquity.
Bless, Lord, we pray Thee, Preses Hoey, [7]
    Serving others, never showy.
On these Thy gifts Thy blessings pour,
    That we may praise Thee more and more.

***

[6] David MacVicar
[7] Preses from the Latin praeses: protector, quardian, president. Graham Hoey, business-
man, Cathedral elder, active in Rotary, Trades House, Order of St. John, and Freemasonry.

The people of Antiquity,
    As anyone may read
Were active in iniquity,
    In thought and word and deed.

But those in this Society,
    We confidently say,
Are pillars of Propriety,
    At home, at work, at play.

Bless, Lord, their kind providing,
    Before us, richly spread,
And by Thy Spirit's guiding
    May they and we be led.

***

God our Father, here we gather,
    Thee to praise.
Thou alone truly Antique,
Wilt hear us who Thy blessing seek –
    Ancient of Days.

Thou for one hundred years hast led
Us, both our living and our dead.
Grant, Lord, that we and ours be fed
    Now and always.

***

THE IMPERIAL SOCIETY OF KNIGHTS BACHELOR

Lord, bless the Knights, their ladies fair,
    In this Imperial Society,
And in Thy mercy, hear the prayer
    We offer with sincere propriety.
Bless all our friendships. Do Thou feed
    Our souls and bodies as we each may need.

***

CENTENARY OF THE LAYING OF THE FOUNDATION STONE OF THE CITY CHAMBERS

We thank Thee for this well-laid stone
Which, like a seed with foresight sown,
    Bears fruit still in this place.
Thanks we give Thee for our food,
For everything sent for our good.
    Pray bless us with Thy Grace.

***

A LADIES BUSINESS AND PROFESSIONAL CLUB

Lord, bless this Club
    devoted to Business,
And there is the rub,
    which brings on dizziness.
Some are professional
    ladies, and seeking
In a slightly obsessional
    manner of speaking,
Contacts for work,
    or just to make friends.
What perils may lurk
    here. See it all ends,
After dinner and speeches,
    Lord, blest by Thee,
In contentment that reaches
    the highest degree.

***

THE ST ANDREW SOCIETY, GLASGOW

O Lord, to whom Saint Andrew brought
      A boy with food – more than they could have bought –
Once Thou hadst blessed the five loaves and two fish.
      For Thy gifts here we thank Thee. Bless each dish.

***

O Lord, we thank Thee for making us Scots!
      For, Lord, there are lots
That merit our thanks –
      Having a few of our very own Banks;
And some of our Braes
      Are worthy of praise;
A wealth of fine ballads, poetry, song – It would take far too long
      To thank Thee. We give
Thanks for our food and this land where we live.

***

O Lord! Not bread again, and fish!
      I wish it were some other dish.
Had Andrew brought Thee more resources
      We might have had red meat, rich sauces …

Lord, by Thy grace, make us more humble.
      Even at miracles we'd grumble.
Andrew, bless him, in faith supplied
      Morsels which thousands satisfied.

Grant us Thy grace to be content
      With all these gifts which Thou hast sent.

***

O Thou who kindly didst provide
    The food which Andrew brought,
And with that fare a boy supplied
    Our Lord a wonder wrought.

Lord, though tonight we be but few,
    Bless these Thy gifts, we pray.
All Scots give Thee their thanks most due
    On this Saint Andrew's Day.

***

O Christ, our Lord, to whom Saint Andrew brought
    His brother, Simon, and with him was taught
To catch not fish but men.
    And also brought a boy with loaves and fish
Whereon five thousand fed, as Thou didst wish,
    By means beyond our ken.

Grant us, O Lord, who bring Thee friends and food,
    To know Thy blessing and Thy power for good.

***

O Christ, who with the loaves and fish which Andrew brought,
    Didst feed the hungry crowd who wondered at Thy power:
Bless now our food, and multiply both faith and grace
    In us, who meet in honour of Saint Andrew at this hour.

***

When Thou, O Lord, wouldst give a feast,
    And feed a crowd with resources least,
Andrew, for whom our hearts are glad,
    Brought simple food from a little lad.
Lord, by Thy grace, bless this our food.
    May we follow him, both great and good.

***

Lord Christ, we thank Thee for Saint Andrew
     Who brought to Thee his brother, and who
Brought Thee a boy with loaves and fishes –
     Heavenly food, past human wishes.
Bless now our food. Unite us here
     With friends and kinsfolk far and near.

★★★

Behold us, Lord, well filled with Scottish spirit,
     Yet thirsting still to honour Andrew's name:
Bless us with food and wit, then, by Christ's merit,
     Forgive our sins, and guide us safely hame.

★★★

For everything, from soup to brandy
     We thank Thee, Lord, and for blest Andy;
While, mindful of the loaves and fish,
     We pray Thy blessing on each dish.

★★★

Lord, we pray Thee that it may be
     For us now as for Andrew then –
To hear Thy call, and give our all,
     To serve Thee as fishers of men.

Lord, bless our food. Like the multitude,
     By Thy grace make us satisfied.
To Scots there and here, we pray Thee be near;
     Bless us all this Saint Andrew's-tide.

★★★

In Russia and Greece
    Saint Andrew preached Peace.
The Greeks, to their loss,
    Fixed him to a cross.

That cross all Scots love,
    Still flutters above
Many buildings tonight.
    And that is but right…

For this is his Day
    Lord, hear us, we pray.

To us in this place,
    With our food, give Thy grace.

***

In those far-off days when Andrew was a preacher
    And with Peter and the others spread the Word,
They would sometimes have for dinner
    A new saint or some old sinner,
Andrew's sermons were the best they'd ever heard.

Lord, we know he didn't really come to Scotland,
    For the Russians, Greeks and Turks were his delight,
But on this, his festal day we give thanks for him and say,
    Bless our dinner and us sinners here tonight.

11
The Church

Glasgow Cathedral Annual Dinner

As long ago Saint Mungo came
    To build a church to praise Thy Name,
So we, Thy children in his city,
    Dependent on Thy grace and pity,
Ask Thee to bless us at our dinner,
    Each stumbling saint, each striving sinner,
That we one Family may be,
    United in our love to Thee.

         ***

Father, here we meet again
    Organised by 'Maison Glen'.[1]
Bless everything about this dinner.
    Make it for each of us a winner.

We Thy Family in this place
    Offer Thee these words of Grace.
From us who tread where Mungo trod,
    Thanks and Glory be to God.

         ***

[1] Eric Glen, cathedral elder, and his wife, Ellen organised the cathedral dinner every year, and also the cathedral's not-quite-new shop in the High Street.

Lord, we thank Thee who providest every blessing,
    Food and drink and friendship as we walk life's way.
And we thank Thee for Thy love which keeps us guessing
    As to what will be Thine answer when we pray.

Lord, we thank Thee for the faith which blessed Mungo
    Planted here with fish and bird and tree and bell,[2]
So we pray Thee, give us grace to proclaim Thee in this place,
    And to benefit this city's life as well.

***

Lord we gather for our dinner
    Each a saint and each a sinner.

Give us friendship, sense of humour,
    Banish malice, spiteful rumour.

With Thy blessings on our board
    Give us thankful hearts, good Lord.

***

We thank Thee, Lord, for all Thy gifts both beautiful and good;
    For life, our loved ones, and our friends and, not least, for our food.
Here we are amply blest. A rich supply our table fills.
    And more than that – like Scotland we are rich in Glens and Hills.[3]
Oh, may this Family unite in praise,
    And thank Thee for Thy love through all our days.

***

Behold, O Lord, how good a thing and pleasant
    It might have been tonight to dine off pheasant;
At least a change from never-ending chicken,
    A dish which now can't make our pulses quicken.
But, praise to Thee, it's haunch of venison.
    Give it, O lord, and us, Thy benison.

[2] Fish, bird, tree and bell feature in the legends of St Mungo and in the coat of arms of Glasgow.
[3] Eric and Ellen Glen and Sir Graham and Lady Hills, former Principal of Strathclyde University and cathedral elder.

Thou knowest, Lord, that in the past
      Folk thought it was enough to fast –
That right from this first day of Lent
      Our energies should all be bent
Towards fasting – getting daily thinner.
      Instead of that – we have a DINNER.

Help us then, Lord of all, to see
      That what it is that pleaseth Thee
Is simply to enjoy each gift
      Of Thine, good Lord, and to Thee lift
Our thanks from hearts which know that Thou
      Art here among us now.

★★★

As Saint Mungo long ago
      On fish and bird and tree
Asked the blessing of Thy grace,
      And rang his bell for Thee;
Grant us, O Lord, a blessing here
      On these gifts from Thy hand,
And as we preach and praise Thy Name
      Fulfil Thy least command.

★★★

Lord, it often happens that
      We have come along and sat,
Waiting to receive a treat,
      Wine to drink and food to eat.
We forget the toil and fret
      Of those who've worked before we've met.
So we thank Thee, Lord, for those
      Who long ago our menu chose,
Sold the tickets, filled each table,
      Found entertainers, fit and able.
With thankful hearts we bless again
      Eric, and not less Ellen, Glen.
For all that Thou hast laid before us,
      We lift out hearts in silent chorus.

Some think we should not thank Thee, Lord, in rhyme,
     And yet in church we do it all the time.
Grant then, whatever be our attitude,
     That we be one in offering Thee our gratitude.

For these Thy gifts with which we're really blessed,
     Our heartfelt, faltering praises be expressed.
For welcoming warmth, not coldly esoteric,
     Our thanks we pay to Ellen Glen and Eric.

★★★

Lord, bless our dinner.
     If it makes us not thinner
Let us not be much fatter
     And then it won't matter
For, though it is Lent
     It is all heaven-sent.
May it fit us to be
     Each a witness to Thee.

★★★

Some think we'll all be merrier
     If we drink more than Perrier.
We recall Saint Paul did recommend the wine.
     But for those who think they oughter
Leave it out and stick to water,
     There's the unsurpassed stuff piped from Loch Katrine.

Lord, we've said as much before.
     Thanks to Thee for gifts galore
But before we stop to rest our tongue or pen,
     There are plenty to say Graces
But to put folk in their places
     None can equal Eric, here and Ellen Glen.

★★★

Whether, in pulpit, organ loft, or pew,
        Thou givest to every one of us a view
Of life as Thou wouldst really have it be.
        For grace in Christ, all praise and thanks to Thee,
And for this table for us richly spread
        Our thanks be felt and never merely said.
Let us who walk where Mungo trod,
        As he did, serve and praise our God.

***

12
The Chamber of Commerce

GLASGOW JUNIOR CHAMBER OF COMMERCE COLQUHOUN DINNERS

Patrick Colquhoun (1745-1820), a tobacco merchant who became Lord Provost, was founder and president of Glasgow Chamber of Commerce in 1783. Charles Oakley founded the Junior Chamber and the name Colquhoun was given to their annual dinner.

The graces are mainly for the junior chamber.

This annual dinner can't come too soon,
  And tonight we're even keener
To honour our founder, Patrick Colquhoun,
  And with him our chairman, Catriona.

With graces material and divine
  Our souls and bodies nourish.
Lord, by the wisdom that is Thine,
  Let us and Glasgow flourish.

    ★★★

May commerce bring us some reward,
  Of profit a fair measure,
And food and friends around this board
  Fill all our hearts with pleasure.

We thank Thee for Thy goodness, Lord,
  That joys grow more, not fewer.
Now full support may all accord
  To our chairman, David Muir.

    ★★★

Lord, we here are richly blest,
    Generous host and willing guest,
With these good things here provided
    By Thy hand which long hath guided
Commerce in this place we love.
    Praise we all our God above
For Colquhoun, name we revere.
    May his work inspire us here.

***

Lord, we've no lack of folk to look back
    And tell us of Dale and Colquhoun; [1]
But here by thy grace in this noble place
    We crave of Thee one greater boon.

From Thee cometh food and everything good,
    And wisdom. Give us grace to heed it.
Give us the vision, the will, the decision
    To make history, not just to read it.

***

[1] David Dale, of humble Ayrshire origin, eventually became a cotton manufacturer and founding vice-president of the Chamber of Commerce.

95

O God, our Father, at the start we
    Pray for our Chairman, Tom McCartney.
For him and his company, we pray –
    Thou knowest, Lord – MB Longmuir & Hay.

For Chartered Quantity Surveyors
    In general, we offer Thee our prayers.
But with our economy prone to fractures
    Grant us an upturn in manufactures.
Give greater incentives for Construction,
    (They would like a V-A-T reduction!)
Grant us more faith for, like St Thomas,
    There are some with doubts in the Chamber of Commerce.

Thanks be to Thee for Thy gifts, O Lord.
    Thy Name we praise with one accord.

***

Charles Oakley, MacLean, James Aitken, MacLeod,
    A P Robertson too, O Lord, must be proud.[2]
This Chamber they founded – the year thirty-seven –
    Thy Spirit hath guided with wisdom from heaven.

Bless, Lord, their successors and their projects four –
    Materials for Castlemilk children who draw;
Helping school-leavers apply for a job;
    Advice on finance careers, worth a few bob;
Books for school libraries, funds from the Bank
    Of Scotland whom we, as its lifelong friends, thank.

For this food and our fellowship we all thank Thee,
    And I, for her help, Chamber's Karen McGhee.[3]

***

[2] Founders in 1937 of the Junior Chamber.
[3] Karen McGhee, then in the Chamber of Commerce office, provided the information on Castlemilk.

Now this ageing Junior Chamber is touching fifty-five,
　　　But their sprightly Founder Chairman, Charles, is very much alive.
So Lord, we ask Thy blessing as we come at the behest
　　　Of our Chairman, Duncan Tannahill who has welcomed every guest.
Bless this food for us, O Lord, let not the evening end too soon,
　　　Nor our reverent gratitude grow dim for the great Patrick Colquhoun.

★★★

We all too soon
　　　shall be forgotten
like Patrick Colquhoun
　　　With the coming of cotton.

But Thou, the all-loving and all-wise
　　　gav'st him Success Through Enterprise.

Likewise, O Lord, bless Nial McClure.
　　　May he and all whom he leads be sure
of Thy grace not only blessing their meat,
　　　but also smoothing life's path for their feet.

★★★

AMERICAN CHAMBER OF COMMERCE INAUGURAL LUNCH

Business seldom is romantic,
　　　Bless, then, those with wider vision.
Bless this chamber Transatlantic,
　　　Further every wise decision;
As these gifts before us spread,
　　　So by Thee may we be led.

★★★

13
Motoring

RSAC General Committee Dinner

The Royal Scottish Automobile Club has been a welcome place where men and woman meet, talk and dine. Accommodation for overnight visitors is available. The club is responsible for organising rallies, and has a magnificent collection of trophies.

Motto: 'Gang Warily'

Thou knowest, Lord, how blest folk are
    Since Thou hast given them THE CAR.
But where to eat? Ah, there's the rub!
    Except for us who have this Club.

To run it well, Lord, in Thy pity
    Thou gav'st this General Committee.
For all Thy gifts – this table spread –
    From lead-free hearts our thanks be said.

        ***

Lord, whatever 'trials' come,
    Thou dost help us 'rally' –
Laxford Bridge to Coldingham,
    Arbroath to Dalmally.

Fuel all our travelling
    With Thine untaxed Spirit,
Complex rules unravelling,
    More than we can merit.

Bless our food, Lord, and our wine.
    Grace our table as we dine.

        ***

Thanks, Lord, for the RSAC,
　　Bless us with this dinner,
Tasty dishes, speeches racy,
　　Make it, Lord, a winner!
In our journeys near and far
　　We shall bless Thee for THE CAR.

***

Help us 'Gang Warily',
　　Not driving 'hairily'.
May we dine merrily,
　　Praising Thee verily.

***

　　Lord, we pray, in all our driving
　　Keep us free from selfish striving,
And bring honour to this Club in every way.
　　Let us eat and drink together,
　　And forget about the weather,
Let Thy presence bless us all, O Lord, we pray.

　　Any of us at this juncture
　　May be suffering a puncture.
Keep our minds from all misfortunes such as this.
　　Grant a miracle of air,
　　Or a heaven-sent repair.
Lord, Thy blessing here will fill us all with bliss.

***

Help us 'Gang Warily',
　　With care, not airily
Forcing the rest to the side.
　　Help us dine merrily,
Thanking Thee verily
　　For all that Thy love doth provide.

***

Lord, we thank Thee for the pleasure
Thou hast given in fullest measure
To each one of us who loves to drive a car.
It would not be very nice
To complain of fog and ice,
For by these we learn the skills to travel far.

So we pray Thee, Lord, to guide us.
On the road of life provide us
With the wisdom and the courtesy we need.
Bless our friendship and this board.
And for all Thy goodness, Lord
May our gratitude be shown in word and deed

★★★

O Lord, we pray Thee, bless this Club,
That it may always be the hub –
The meeting place of many spokes,
Like us and many other folks.

Of all such places in our city,
Thanks to the General Committee,
This Club of ours is unsurpassed.
And while in Lent we ought to fast,
We pray Thee bless our food and drink.
They're gifts of Thine, we like to think.
Now we who've come from near or far
Thank Thee for giving us The Car.

★★★

Help us go with care
In the many joys we share,
Taking pleasure in the comfort of this place.
Both behind the wheel,
And at this and every meal,
Grant to us, O Lord, the blessings of Thy grace.

★★★

Bless us, Father, when we drive,
  Keep us and all we meet alive.
Bless this Club, guide this Committee.
  May their work enhance our city.
By Thy Spirit, and this table
  For Thy service make us able.

***

O Lord, there's nothing like a car
  For quite short trips, or going far
Beyond the confines of the city.
  although it seems to be a pity
That often, just at such a juncture,
  One finds one has sustained a puncture.

At such a time one's almost fated
  To find one's spare's not been inflated,
And many miles may separate
  One from a phone. Well, one can wait,
Enjoy the scenery in peace,
  Or send smoke signals for the Police.

Lord, bless this Club, the R-S-A-C.
  Here, we the past and future may see,
With speakers wise, whose stories witty
  Are shorter than this devious ditty.

O bless this meal and grant that we
  For everything give thanks to Thee.

***

CENTENARY DINNER

Lord, who hast given us the Car,
      We have got too many, far,
We sometimes wish that we had powers
      To scrap all others, just keep ours.
While Thou hast faced us with the question,
      How to answer Road Congestion?
Maker of varied scenery,
      Bless us on our Centenary.
Bless our meal, Lord. Grant that we
      For all Thy gifts give thanks to Thee.

★★★

RSAC SCOTTISH SONGS NIGHTS

Lord, Thou Giver of all good,
      Please draw near to bless
Us and this good Scottish food,
      And our Highland dress.

Whether we're from North or South,
      Be with us, we pray.
Direct the traffic of each mouth,
      All we eat or say.

Bless this land from which we're sprung,
      Her folk from Leith to Luss;
And when her praises we have sung
      May she be proud of us.

★★★

DINNER FOR RETIREMENT OF ROBERT TENNANT REID,
MC, CHIEF EXECUTIVE

Lord, we thank Thee for this evening, and the reason
    Why we've met to show our love and thanks to Bob.
First, we thank Thee for this dinner
    (which won't make us any thinner!)
Then we thank Thee that he's done a marvellous job.

He has made this Club a home from home for many,
    With his friendship, patience, humour, we've been blest.
And he's helped remove the striving
    From our ordinary driving,
While each Rally's been a pleasure and a test!

On his own, he might have found the task much harder,
    So we thank Thee, Lord, for giving him Janette.
Now on both the Tennant Reids
    Who have cared for all our needs
May the sunshine of Thy loving never set.

***

14
Police

STRATHCLYDE POLICE CHARITY DINNER

O God, put us all in the mood
    To give Thee thanks for our food
Which Thy love and grace doth provide.
    But elsewhere tonight, far and wide
In Strathclyde, the rest of our Force
    Are busy on duty, of course.
Perhaps, Lord, never before
    Have we given Thee thanks for John Orr,
For him who is Chief.
    And What a relief
That most of the bucks stop with him,
    Or with Deputy Jim,
Who surveys us tonight from the Chair,
    Making sure the proceedings are fair.
That we all, both the bold and the brave,
    Give freely the Children to Save.
With Thy blessing provided tonight,
    Let us help make their future bright.

***

O Lord, before we eat and drink,
    Grant by Thy grace, that we may think
Of little children who can't walk,
    Or wave their arms, or even talk.
Or those, as eventide descends,
    Who find in Age Concern good friends.
Bless, Lord, this food to keep us living,
    And move our hearts, and hands, to giving.
Then, after braveheart words from Wallace,[1]
    Grant us Thy peace to be our solace.

***

[1] Guest speaker, Deputy First Minister James Wallace.

ASSOCIATION OF CHIEF POLICE OFFICERS OF SCOTLAND

Lord, bless this Association –
    Chiefs, their guests, our conversation.
While others have to pound the beat,
    Bless, O Lord, the food we eat.
For all the gifts which Thou hast given,
    We thank Thee, Lord of earth and heaven.

***

CRIME STOPPERS DINNER

Bless all those, Lord, who give their time
    And energies to stopping crime.
Bless each anonymous report
    Through which offenders may be caught.
Bless speakers here, like Annabel,
    Who came last year, and spoke so well,
Experienced, but not an oldie,
    Although unquestionably Goldie.
Bless Messrs Vannet and McKay
    Dispensing Justice from on high,
And John Orr, Chief here in Strathclyde,
    Although Kilmarnock is his pride.
Lord, with all these speakers Thou has blest us.
    May each and every speech arrest us.
Of Thy love, Lord, there is no question.
    Please give us all a good digestion.

***

15
Graces Written for Others to Say

EVENING TIMES WOMAN OF THE YEAR AWARD LUNCH
(delivered by Dr Jean Morris)

Almighty God who, by Thy grace
      Dost give us each a special place,
May we, while thanking Thee for Man,
      Give thanks to Thee that in Thy plan
Thou dost proved these blessings here
      And, too, a Woman of the Year,
Who by her work our sights may raise
      To aim for heights which give Thee praise.
Grant us Thy blessing. May we give
      Our gifts in service while we live.

***

(also delivered by Dr Jean Morris)

We thank Thee, Lord, who gather here
      For the 'Scotswoman of the Year'.
May she inspire us so to live
      That we to Thee our best may give.
Bless now our friendships and our food,
      Praise to Thee, Giver of all good.

***

SOUNDAROUND
(Wireless for the Hard of Hearing)
For John Whitney, Director General, IBA

Father, whose good gifts abound,
  Thou hast given us Soundaround.
For the friendships thus engendered
  Thanks to Thee by all be tendered.
On us and these good gifts supplied
  let Thy grace be multiplied.

THE PRINCE'S TRUST AND DUKE OF EDINBURGH AWARDS
Graces offered to Ronnie Corbett at his request for an event in February 1996.

We give thanks to Thee, as we certainly must
  For the work of The Prince's Trust,
For the Duke of Edinburgh Awards,
  And the opportunities each affords
To the energetic youth of our nation
  In every successive generation.
Now bless, Lord, we pray, these gifts provided.
  May we all evermore by Thee be guided.

     ***

O God, our Father in heaven,
  We, The Magnificent Seven
And others, eager and bright,
  Who with us this evening unite,
Give thanks, as we certainly must,
  For the work of The Prince's Trust
And the Duke of Edinburgh Award.
  Now we ask Thee to bless, O Lord,
These gifts of Thy grace on each table.
  We pray that they will enable
Us all to further this work.
  This challenge let none of us shirk.

     ***

50TH ANNIVERSARY OF THE JOINT COMMITTEE OF THE RAC, THE AA AND THE RSAC
For the Chairman of the RSAC

O Lord, we thank Thee in this ditty
    That Thou hast blessed our Joint Committee –
The RAC, Lord, and the AA
    Who help the motorist on the highway.
In Scotland too where any may see
    Rallies run by the RSAC.
We thank Thee for this food provided.
    For fifty more years may we be guided.

***

16

Graces for the Queen's Body Guard for Scotland Royal Company of Archers

For teaching us Thy will to know,
    To judge 'twixt wrong and right;
For him who fashioned the first bow,
    Watched the first arrow's flight.

For food and drink, and each good gift
    For each returning Spring,
Our thanks, O Lord, to Thee we lift,
    Our hearts Thy praises sing.

***

Not every wood,
    O Lord, we know,
Is any good
    To make a bow.

But thou dost choose
    Each son of Thine,
Each Thou canst use
    In his own line

Bless, Lord, this food,
    That it and we,
Be doing good
    By serving thee.

***

Let Thine arrows fly, and find
    Their mark within man's mind;
And his words and deeds inspire,
    With flashes of Thy fire.
Archers with food and friendship bless.
    To Thee, Lord we our praise address.

***

Some pray for bows of burning gold,
    And arrows of desire;
Ambition, daring, dreams untold
    Such mighty deeds imspire.
But for contentment, daily bread,
    With friends at close of day
For these gifts, Lord, our thanks be said,
    And bless us all we pray.

***

Lord, help us aim
    Not for honours and fame,
Nor for trivial prize
    But aim for the skies,
Be approved in Thine eyes,
    And so hit the clout
Before time runs out.
    Bless our food, with our friends,
Before the day ends.

***

We pray Thee, Lord, to revive
      And help Archers relax from the rigour
Of shooting and having to strive
      For this fine Claret Jug of Biggar.[1]
Bless our food and our friendship, we pray,
      As we give Thee thanks for this day.

★★★

Lord, we are ' come to drink the wine ...
      On the bonny banks o' Yarrow,'[2]
To meet good friends of auld lang syne
      And shoot for the Selkirk Arrow.

And though we've not all 'licked the birse,'
      Bless our friends and our food we pray,
As we give Thee thanks in our humble verse
      Foe all that's been good today.

★★★

Lord, from hearts both warm and loyal,
      We pray Thee bless the Princess Royal,
Who her target never misses,
      Carefully takes aim, and this is
Saving Children, those denied
      By handicap will learn to ride;
Carers needing respite care,
      Find her ever ready there.
Bless, with these gifts, our newest bristle –
      The latest Lady of the Thistle.

★★★

[1] The Royal Company of Archers visit Selkirk, Biggar and other places in Scotland, some annually and some less often, to shoot for prizes given to the Royal Company long ago, which include the Selkirk Arrow and the Claret Jug (of Biggar).
[2] The quotation referring to Yarrow is from Sir Walter Scott, himself a member of the Royal Company. To 'lick the birse' was part of the Yarrow Freedom Ceremony in which the new Freeman would dip a bristle in his wine and then drink it.

Only 'a fool i' the forest,
 A motley fool' could sigh,
'Ay, now am I in Arden,
 The more fool I.'[3]

For our friends the Woodmen of Arden,
 Our thanks, O Lord, we bring.
Whose home is a green leafy garden,
 Where their arrows sing.

Their arrows fly in Arden,
 As ours at Holyrood.
For winning we ask their pardon,
 And thank Thee for our food.[4]

   ***

[3] The quotations in this grace of 1997 are from Shakespeare's *As You Like It*.
[4] The match against the English archers, the Woodmen of Arden, takes place every three years, alternately in the grounds of the Palace of Holyroodhouse, and at Arden in Warwickshire.

List of Subscribers

Henry C Abram
A J Blair Agnew
Ronald Ainsworth
J Douglas Anderson
S Lothian Barclay
Sheila Best
James H Black
Murray S Blair
John J Blanche
Alexander A H Bone
Lucille Bone
Kenneth E L Brown
Ian D Brown
Alistair S Burrow
Ann Caldwell
Joseph J Caldwell
Arlene Cambridge
James H Campbell
J Stewart Couper
John G Craig
W G Crichton
Allison E Denholm
Avril E Denholm
J Allan Denholm
J Keith Denholm
Wallace Dick
Professor Geoffrey R Dixon
Richmond Douglas
Annette K Drummond Young
P Rory Duff
David Dunbar

Ian L Dunsmore
John O Elliott
John G Fergus
Alan Ferguson
Fletcher Jones Limited
David Forrester
Martin B F Frame
James P Fyfe
Matthew M Garrey
Thomas Gilchrist
Graham Goodridge Cox
William N Gordon
David C Grahame
John Hay
D I Henderson
S Graham Hoey
Brian A Holmes
Ragne Hopkins
Hugh M K Hopkins
Charlotte Horspool
George B Horspool
Peter G Howie
Archibald S Hunter
Richard J A Hunter
J Mitchell Hutcheson
Sir Peter Hutchison
Roy A Johnson
Gordon H Kee
Hugh Kelly
Jean P Kelso
Peter S Kelso

Jonathan Edward Kinghorn
A Harith Kulasinghe
Peter M Kyle
G Alastair Lean
Ralph & Mary Leishman
J Michael Low
Ian MacConnacher
George McCulloch
Keith W Macintosh
Iain Macfarlane
G Rutherford Macfarlane
John MacKenzie
Avril MacLeod
Ian A Macpherson
John C Maginnis
Angela Matheson
Jamie G Matheson
G Michael McChlery
Judith H McDowell
Anne McFadden
Alastair J McLay
David R McMillan
James P S McNeill
Bette B Millar
David & Fiona Millar
James Morrison
William Morrison
Ewan S Murray
John B Park
Craig Paterson

Rona & Frank Potter
Allan Ramsay
Robert Ramsey
John A Reid
A William Richardson
David M Richmond
Ian C Ritchie
T Iain Robertson
Robert W K C Rogerson
David A Roser
Kenneth E Sandford
Michael J Sandford
Aileen Scott
Ian J Scott
Janette Scott
Jean Scott
Roy Scott
Ian B Smail
Sir Robert & Lady Smith
John R Steele
J Neilson Stevenson
Robert G Strathdee
David Watson
Alan J Watt
Ian M Will
Peter D Winton
T Malcolm T Wishart
Gordon M Wyllie
Harry S Wylie
Harry L Yeomans